FORCES AND MACHINES

OTHER BOOKS BY ROBERT GARDNER

A FRANKLIN INSTITUTE SCIENCE MUSEUM BOOK

INVESTIGATE AND DISCOVER
FORCES AND MACHINES

ROBERT GARDNER

JULIAN MESSNER

Copyright © 1991 by Robert Gardner
Illustrations © 1991 by Robert R. Jackson

All rights reserved including the right of reproduction in
whole or in part in any form.
Published by Julian Messner, a division of Silver Burdett
Press, Inc., Simon & Schuster, Inc., Prentice Hall Bldg.,
Englewood Cliffs, NJ 07632.
JULIAN MESSNER and colophon are trademarks
of Simon & Schuster, Inc.
Design by Leslie Bauman.

10 9 8 7 6 5 4 3 2 1 (lib. ed.)
10 9 8 7 6 5 4 3 2 1 (paper ed.)

Library of Congress Cataloging-in-Publication Data

Gardner, Robert.
Forces and machines / Robert Gardner.
p. cm.—(Investigate and discover)
Includes bibliographical references and index.
Summary: Explores forces and machines through a variety of
experiments and hands-on activities.
1. Force and energy—Juvenile literature.   2. Force and energy—
Experiments—Juvenile literature.   3. Simple machines—Juvenile
literature.   4. Science museums—Educational aspects—Juvenile
literature.   [1. Force and energy—Experiments.   2. Simple
machines—Experiments.   3. Experiments.]   I. Title.   II. Series.
QC73.4G37   1991
531′.6—dc20   91-24564
                                                                 CIP
                                                                  AC

ISBN 0-671-69041-8 (LSB)   ISBN 0-671-69046-9 (pbk.)

▲▲▲▲▲▲▲▲▲▲▲

CONTENTS

▲▲▲▲▲▲▲▲▲▲▲

THE SCIENCE MUSEUM AT THE FRANKLIN INSTITUTE

The Franklin Institute in Philadelphia was founded more than 150 years ago and is named for Benjamin Franklin, one of the United States' first experimental scientists. The Franklin Institute was the first hands-on science center in the country and each year plays host to thousands of people of all ages curious about both new and old discoveries in science and technology.

In preparing this book and other books in the Investigate and Discover series, the author and publisher have made extensive use of the exhibits and facilities in the Science Museum, Fels Planetarium, and Futures Center at the Institute. Some of the photographs that appear in the books were taken at the Institute, and many of the investigations and features in the books are related to exhibits you can see and things you can do there.

The author and publisher appreciate the cooperation of the Franklin Institute staff in helping to develop some of the material in this series. Like the author, the staff believe that the way to understand science is to do it.

▲▲▲▲▲▲▲▲▲▲▲

INTRODUCTION: DOING SCIENCE

Have you ever wondered what causes a great thunderstorm, or how brakes stop a car, or why a satellite orbits the earth? These are the kinds of mysteries that science can explain.

Of course, it's good to use books to look up answers, but another way of learning is by "doing science"—observing and figuring out answers for yourself. That's actually the way scientists work. They observe carefully, take notes, search for more information if needed, and then come up with answers.

You can discover a great deal about the physical world especially if you have the right attitude. Be curious. Keep asking yourself why the things taking place right around you are happening. Another great way to learn and take part in activities that explain the world is to visit a science museum. Don't miss any chance you get to do so. You might go with your class or with your family or friends. There you'll find exhibits that are fascinating to look at and to work with.

The experiments you can do with this book can help you to have some of the same kinds of adventures at home or at school. Try the experiments and you can become part of the world of science. You can begin to think like a scientist and learn the way a scientist does. Here are some useful tips.

As you experiment or visit a museum, keep a notebook by your side. If possible, use a notebook that has graph paper on at least some pages. Graphs and diagrams will then be easy to draw. When you make an observation or do an experiment, record the facts in your notebook. When a new idea comes to mind, write that down, too. Be sure to include the details of experiments that don't work out. Errors and failed experiments can lead to new insights, and then often to success.

Safety First

Experimenting sometimes involves using materials that can be dangerous if they aren't used the right way. Always keep these points in mind:

▼Let a teacher, parent, or other responsible adult know that you're going to experiment.

▼Read all instructions carefully. If you have questions, check with the adult. Don't take chances.

▼Whether you work with a friend or alone, maintain a serious attitude when experimenting. Horseplay could be dangerous to you and others.

▼Substances can be poisonous. Don't taste anything unless instructed to do so.

▼Keep the area where you are experimenting clean and well organized. When you've finished, clean up and put all the materials away.

▼Never experiment with electricity in wall outlets.

And now let's find out what we can discover about the fascinating subject of forces and machines.

▲▲▲▲▲▲▲▲▲▲

LET'S GET MOVING!

The subject of motion has been of interest to people for thousands of years. Aristotle, a Greek philosopher who lived in the fourth century B.C., made one of the earliest studies of how and why things move. One of the conclusions he reached was that an object will not move unless something is pushing or pulling it. That is, it won't move unless a force is acting on it. Once that force stops acting, the object will stop moving. Aristotle also said that the speed of an object (the distance it travels per unit time) depends on the size or strength of the force acting on it. A big force will make an object move fast. With a small force, the same object will move slowly.

You may think that all this makes sense. After all, objects such as chairs do not move unless something causes them to do so. When you push a chair, you make it move. When you stop pushing, it stops moving. If you push hard, it moves fast. If you apply a small push, it moves slowly. However, not all pushes produce motion. If the push you apply to the chair is very small, for example, the chair doesn't move at all. Aristotle gave a sensible explanation for this fact as well. He said it takes a certain minimum amount of force to overcome a special force that acts between two objects that rub against each other, such as a chair and the floor—a force called *friction*. However, before you jump onto Aristotle's bandwagon and assume that his explanations of motion are correct, try Investigation 1–1.

▲▲▲▲▲▲▲▲▲▲▲

INVESTIGATION 1–1: A FRICTIONLESS AIR CAR

Materials needed: saw · small piece of ¼-in. plywood · fine sandpaper · drill and bit (¹/₁₆-in.) · wooden spool · glue · medium-to-large balloon · small nail · hammer · smooth jar top

You will be building a simple air car. Sets of directions are given for two slightly different cars.

First Design (Figure 1–1a, steps 1–4).

1. Ask an adult to cut a 3-in. (7.5-cm) square from the ¼-in. plywood.

2. Have an adult use the ¹/₁₆-in. drill to make a hole in the center of the wood square.

3. Use the fine sandpaper to smooth the bottom and round the edges of the square.

4. Line up the hole in the wooden spool with the hole in the wood square. Then use the glue to attach the spool to the square. Let dry. Blow up the balloon and pull the neck over the end of the spool. The figure accompanying step 4 shows the finished air car.

Second Design (Figure 1–1b, steps 1–3).

1. Use the small nail and the hammer to punch a small hole in the center of the top side of the smooth jar top.

2. Line up the hole in the spool with the hole in the jar top. Use the glue to attach the spool to the bottom side of the jar top.

3. Inflate the balloon and pull its neck over the end of the spool. The figure accompanying step 3 shows the finished air car.

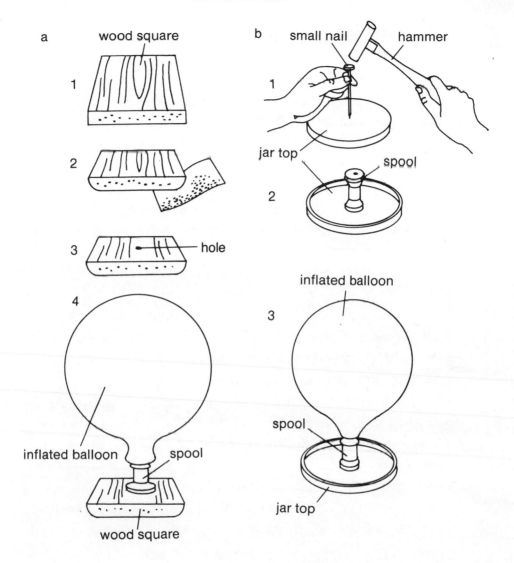

FIGURE 1-1 *Plans for two simple air cars that can be used to investigate motion.*

Place the air car on a very smooth table or counter top and give it a little push. Notice how it glides along. Is its speed fairly constant or does it slow down very quickly when you are no longer pushing it? Once it is moving, do you have to keep pushing to make it continue to move? What do you have to do to make it move faster? To make it stop?

Galileo Takes a Different View

After observing the air car, you may have some doubts about Aristotle's ideas. You probably found that the car, once started, keeps on moving, even when there is no longer any force acting on it. According to Aristotle, this sort of thing should not happen. But it did! Something must, therefore, be wrong with his reasoning.

In the sixteenth century, Galileo Galilei (1564-1642), the Italian scientist often called the father of modern science, also questioned Aristotle's explanation of motion. He agreed with Aristotle that an object at rest (stationary) will not move unless a force acts on it. However, Galileo differed from Aristotle on another point. The Italian scientist believed that an object in motion will continue to move rather than slow down in the absence of a force. It will slow down and finally stop only if a force that opposes its motion acts on it.

Galileo observed, as you can, that when a ball is thrown, the ball continues to move after it leaves the hand. Galileo also observed that if a ball is thrown straight up, it rises, slows down, stops momentarily, and falls back to Earth. Instead of assuming that the ball, when no longer pushed upward, "runs out of steam," so to speak, he reasoned that something causes the ball to slow down. Thus, unlike Aristotle, he did not assume that only motion needs an explanation, whereas slowdown is "natural" to unpushed objects and therefore needs no explanation. He believed that the earth is the cause of the change in motion of a rising ball. According to Galileo, the earth pulls on the ball, making it slow down and finally stop. Since the earth's pull on the ball is continuous, the ball, after stopping at the top of its path, will fall back to Earth. The earth exerts a force on the ball. This force is one that you're undoubtedly very familiar with; it's called *gravity*.

Galileo was not able to explain *why* the earth should pull

(attract) everything toward it. (Incidentally, no one has ever explained why gravity does this.) But you certainly have good evidence that he was right about the earth's ability to pull on things. All you have to do is drop an object and watch it fall toward the earth. Or try to jump as high as you can.

Galileo claimed that once an object is set in motion, it will continue to move unless a force acts on it. He believed that the reason most objects stop moving when you stop pushing on them is that friction causes them to slow down. The legs of a sliding chair, for example, rub against the floor. This provides a frictional force that quickly brings the chair to rest. A ball, on the other hand, will roll for a long time after you release it because there is very little friction between the ball and the floor. A baseball, a cannon ball, or an arrow shot from a bow will all continue to move long after the force that started them moving has been removed.

With all this in mind, Galileo carried out what is known as a thought experiment. He imagined a ball rolling down a short but *frictionless* incline. Since there was no friction to stop the ball, he said the ball would continue to move when it reached the level surface at the bottom of the incline. If the ball reached another incline a short distance away, it would roll upward to a height equal to the height from which it started, as shown in Figure 1–2*a*. If the second incline were farther from the original incline (as in Figure 1–2*b*), the ball would simply travel farther on the level part of its journey. On a surface parallel to the earth's surface, and without any second hill at all, the ball would continue to move forever (Figure 1–2*c*). With no force to stop or slow down an object, it continues to move. Once again, motion needs no explanation. Only *changes* in motion require an explanation.

To illustrate his thought experiment, Galileo used a pendulum. The pendulum bob (the weight at the bottom) moves like the ball he imagined in his thought experiment. You'll have a chance to see just how a pendulum moves in the next investigation.

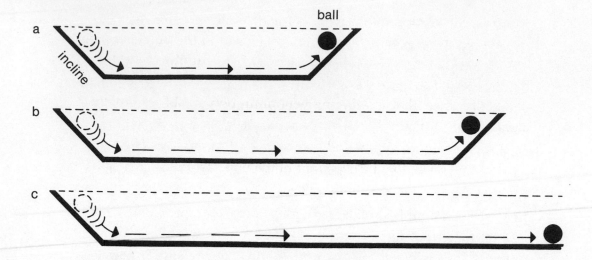

FIGURE 1-2 *In a thought experiment, Galileo imagined a ball moving along a very long, flat, frictionless surface in three different situations.*

▲▲▲▲▲▲▲▲▲▲▲
INVESTIGATION 1–2: A PENDULUM

Materials needed: tongue depressor · tape · several heavy steel washers · string · two rulers · clothespins · clock or watch with second hand, or stopwatch

You can build a simple pendulum like the one shown in Figure 1–3. **Ask an adult to use a sharp knife or a razor blade to make a slit about 1 in. (2–3 cm) long in the tongue depressor.** Tape the tongue depressor to the top of a door frame, a high shelf, or a table. Attach one of the heavy steel washers to the end of the string. The washer will serve as the pendulum bob. Slide the string through the slit in the tongue depressor. Pull the bob to one side, let go, and watch it swing back and forth. (If the string slips through the slit in the tongue depressor, tape the string above the slit to the top of the depressor.)

The back-and-forth motion helps illustrate Galileo's thought experiment. Gravity pulls on the bob and makes it swing downward from the top of its arc to the lowest point in its swing. But then, even though gravity is pulling the bob straight downward, the bob continues to move and swings upward to the other end of the arc. Is the height to which it swings equal to the height from which it was released, as Galileo predicted? Set up the two rulers held by the clothespins as shown in Figure 1-3 and find out.

Galileo knew that a swinging pendulum bob would eventually stop. That's because there is friction between the bob and the air and between the string and its support. To see the effect of friction, measure the initial height of the bob and then the height it reaches after a few swings. How do the two heights of swing compare? If there were no friction, how high would the later swing be?

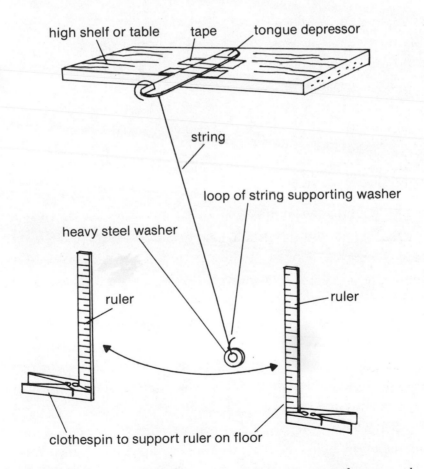

FIGURE I-3 *With the pendulum shown here, you can perform a number of interesting experiments.*

Though Galileo used a pendulum mainly to illustrate his idea that bodies in motion continue to move, he was also interested in the pendulum itself. He noticed that its back-and-forth motion seemed to have a certain steadiness or regularity about it. He decided to investigate the pendulum's *period*—that is, the time that it takes a pendulum to make one complete swing and return to its initial position. You will attempt to do this next. It is difficult to measure the time of one swing of the pendulum very accurately, however. To improve the accuracy, you can measure the time it takes the pendulum to make twenty swings. Then divide the total time you measure by the number of swings. Use the clock or watch with a second hand or the stopwatch to measure time. (Galileo used his pulse as a timer. When he lived, clocks could not measure short time intervals.) For example, if the pendulum makes twenty swings in 15 seconds, its period (the time for one swing) must be

$$\frac{15s}{20} = \frac{3}{4}s, \text{ or } 0.75s,$$

where s stands for seconds.

One of the things Galileo investigated next was the way the length of the pendulum affects its period. You can do this, too. Make the pendulum shorter by pulling the string up through the support. What happens to the period when the pendulum is shortened? What happens to the period when you make the pendulum longer?

Does the period of the pendulum change as it swings? Is its period different after fifty swings than it was after ten swings?

Does the period of a pendulum depend on the weight of the bob? Double the weight of the bob by adding another washer to the one you have been using. Be sure, however, that the length of the pendulum—the distance from the top of the string to the middle of the bob—and also the amplitude—the distance the bob swings—are the same as they were when you used the single washer. If you changed the length and/or amplitude of the pendulum *and* the weight of the bob, you wouldn't know which factor causes a change in the period. In any experiment you do, you must be very careful to change only one factor at a time. How does doubling the weight of the bob affect the period of a pendulum? What do you predict will happen to the period if the weight of the bob is tripled? Then test your prediction. Were you right?

At the Franklin Institute Science Museum, and perhaps at other museums, too, you will find a number of carefully constructed pendulums. There, you can investigate the effect of length, weight, and amplitude (distance of swing) on the period. Even at home, however, you can investigate many of the properties of pendulums that Galileo did. Just carry out the "Exploring" activities that follow.

▲▲▲▲▲▲▲▲▲▲▲

EXPLORING ON YOUR OWN

▼Design an experiment to find out whether the period of a pendulum is affected by the amplitude of the swing. What do you find?

▼Make a pendulum swing in an elliptical (oval) path like the one shown in Figure 1-4*a*. (By the way, satellites follow this sort of elliptical path as they orbit the earth.) Make a rough measurement of the pendulum's amplitude, or total path length. Then have the pendulum swing back and forth in a line the way it normally does. How do the amplitudes for the two swings compare? Measure the period for each kind of path. Is the period of the pendulum affected by the path of the bob?

▼Set up a pair of pendulums side by side, like the ones shown in Figure 1-4*b*. Connect the two pendulums with a drinking straw as shown. Pull one of the bobs to the side and let it go as shown in Figure 1-4*c*. What happens to the second bob as time passes? The other four drawings in Figure 1-4*c* suggest some other things to try. Can you account for what you observe?

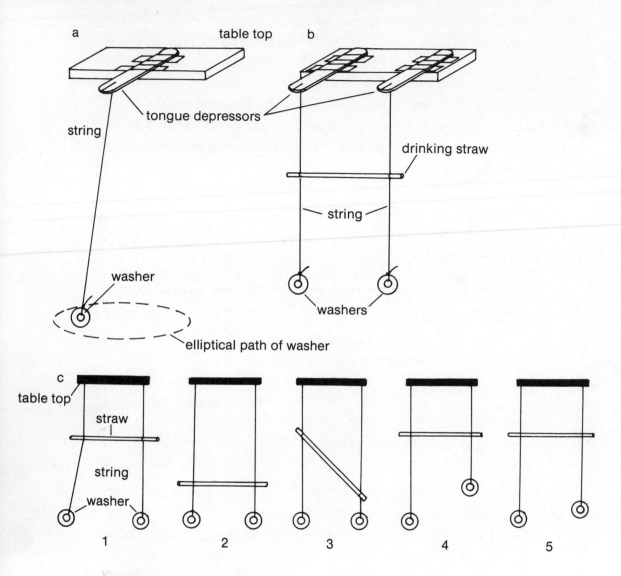

FIGURE 1-4 *Use these diagrams to investigate the elliptical paths of single pendulums (a) and the properties of dual pendulums (b and c).*

▼A playground swing moves like a pendulum. Find out whether the period of the swing is constant. Then try to predict whether the period of the swing will be affected by the weight of a person on the swing or by the length of the swing. Now test your predictions. Were you right?

▼Experiment to find out whether halving the length of a pendulum causes the period to halve. If you reduce the length of a pendulum to one-quarter its former length, what happens to the period? From your results, see whether you can figure out a way to double the period of a pendulum.

▼Support a bicycle in an upside-down position. Give the front wheel a good pull to set it in motion. Does the wheel continue to move after you stop pulling? Is there much friction in the bearings of the wheel?

Objects at Rest

A body in motion keeps on moving at a steady rate unless a force makes it speed up or slow down. Suppose a body is stationary. Will it tend to remain at rest? You can find the answer to this question by carrying out the next investigation.

▲▲▲▲▲▲▲▲▲▲▲

INVESTIGATION 1–3: OBJECTS AT REST

Materials needed: file card · wide-mouthed jar · a quarter and several nickels · marble · narrow-mouthed bottle · paper · plastic cup · water · blocks of wood · hammer · two rulers

Cut the file card in half. Place the card on the mouth of the wide-mouthed jar. Place the quarter or one of the nickels at the center of the card. Then, with a snap of your finger, give the card a sharp push as shown in Figure 1–5a. What happens to the coin? Did it tend to remain at rest?

Repeat the experiment with the marble at the center of the file card placed over the mouth of the narrow-mouthed bottle. Be sure to give the card a sharp push with a snap of your finger. Does the marble behave as the coin did?

Next, place a strip of the paper on a smooth table or counter so that it hangs over the edge. Put the plastic cup half-filled with water on the paper. Pull the end of the paper strip gently toward you, as shown in Figure 1–5b. The cup will move with the paper,

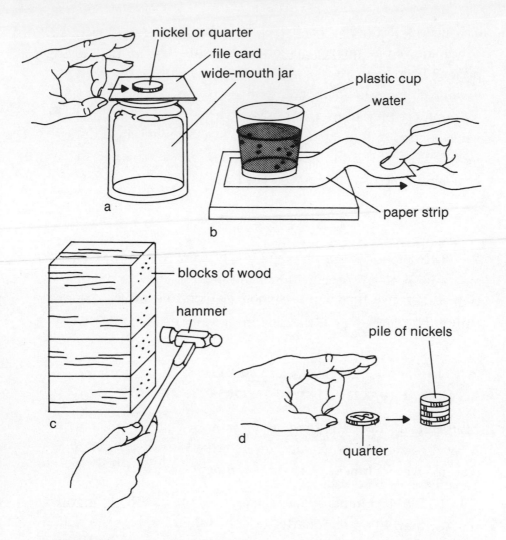

FIGURE 1-5 *Do objects tend to "stay put"? These experiments will help you answer this question.*

as you would expect. Now give the end of the paper strip a quick, strong, sharp pull downward. What happens to the cup of water?

Next, build a "tower," using a number of the blocks of wood. Then use the hammer to apply a sudden sharp force to the block second from the bottom, as shown in Figure 1–5c. What happens to the block you hit? Do the other blocks tend to remain in place? Carry out a similar experiment by flicking the quarter into a small pile of the nickels, as shown in Figure 1–5d. (This will require some practice because it's not easy to make a coin hit straight on.) Use the rulers to serve as guide rails for the moving quarter.

Based on your observations, do objects that are at rest tend to stay at rest?

▲▲▲▲▲▲▲▲▲▲▲
JUST FOR FUN

▼ You may have seen a magician use a tablecloth and dishes to do a trick similar to the experiment shown in Figure 1–5*b*. You might like to try doing this trick for yourself. However, to avoid the danger and expense involved in breaking glass, use plastic dishes. Practice first with a smooth napkin and just one or two dishes. As your technique improves, you can use more dishes and a larger cloth.

The First Law of Motion

Your investigations have probably led you to recognize two very important facts about objects and motion:

1. An object that is moving keeps on moving in a straight line at constant speed unless a force acts on it.
2. An object that is not moving tends to remain at rest unless a force acts on it.

Together these two principles make up what is generally known as Newton's *first law of motion:* An object tends to maintain its state of motion or nonmotion unless acted on by a force. The law was actually first stated by Galileo, but Isaac Newton (1642-1727), who developed it in a more useful form in the 1600s, is generally given credit for it. The law is sometimes called the principle of *inertia.* You can think of inertia as a tendency of objects to resist changes in motion. Like any scientific law, the first law summarizes the results of a vast number of observations and experiments into a single general principle. So far as we know, there are no exceptions to this law.

One common device whose design is based on the first law of motion is the seat belt. These belts, found in airplanes, cars, and trucks, protect the people inside. Now that you have studied motion, you are in a position to understand how these devices work and why they are necessary.

If the driver of a car puts on the brakes, the car slows down. But the driver and any passengers will continue to move with the speed they had before the brakes were applied. The seat belts provide the force needed to keep the people in place. The belts prevent injuries that could occur if the people kept moving and struck the dashboard or windshield.

If you've ridden in a car or an airplane, you've felt the force of a seat belt keeping you in place when the brakes were applied. You've also felt another force—one that was exerted when the speed of the car or plane increased, and that you may not have interpreted correctly. It may have felt as if you were somehow being pushed back into your seat. Actually, you were feeling the force that the back of the seat was exerting on you, pushing you forward to make you speed up. Your body's inertia tended to cause your body to lag behind the change of motion of the vehicle you were in.

By carrying out a few investigations and thinking about the results, you have had a chance to learn a good deal about motion and how forces change motion. In the next chapter, you'll look more closely at the forces needed to make things speed up or slow down. You'll also get to apply what you learn to all sorts of interesting situations and processes that you may have been curious about but never understood.

▼▼▼▼▼▼▼▼▼▼

CHAPTER

2

▲▲▲▲▲▲▲▲▲▲

MOVING RIGHT ALONG

Without a force, a stationary object will remain at rest and a moving object will keep moving at constant speed. Suppose a wagon, skateboard, or some other vehicle is at rest on a level floor or sidewalk. If you briefly apply a constant force that is bigger than the force of friction, you will set the object into motion. But what happens if you continue to apply this same force to the object even after it is moving? Aristotle predicted that the object would move at a steady speed. But will it really behave in this way? The next investigation will help you to answer this question.

▲▲▲▲▲▲▲▲▲▲

INVESTIGATION 2–1: MAKING THINGS MOVE

Materials needed: skateboard or wagon (or a toy truck, toy car, or roller skate) · spring scale or large, long, heavy rubber band and meter stick (or long, thin rubber bands and a ruler) · bricks or weights

Ask a friend to sit on the skateboard or wagon at rest on a level sidewalk or a floor in a large room. Connect the spring scale to the vehicle. Such a scale is used to apply and measure forces. If you don't have a spring scale, you can use a large, heavy rubber band and a meter stick, as shown in Figure 2-1. Pull the vehicle in such a way that you keep the rubber band stretched the same amount all the time you are pulling. Then the force you're using to pull the vehicle will be constant.

Pull very gently on the spring scale or the rubber band and meter stick. How can you estimate the frictional force between the wagon or skateboard and the surface it's on? If you don't have a wagon or skateboard or a large space to work in, you can do a small-scale version of the experiment. Simply use a toy truck, toy car, or roller skate with some bricks or other weights on it. In place of the spring scale or large rubber bands and meter stick, you can use long, thin, rubber bands and a ruler.

Now have another friend hold the vehicle in place while you pull on it with a force several times bigger than the force you need to overcome friction. (The amount of friction is equal to the force you need just to make the vehicle move along very slowly.) When your friend lets go, move along with the vehicle, keeping the spring scale or rubber band stretched the same amount that it was before your friend let go. In this way, you will be applying a constant force to the vehicle.

How does the vehicle move when you pull with a constant force? Does it move at a steady (constant) speed, as Aristotle predicted, or does its speed increase?

What happens if you double the force? You can do this by stretching the spring scale twice as much. (If you're using a rubber band, you can use two rubber bands, each stretched as much as the one you used before.)

Newton and Acceleration

Newton made the same observations that you did in Investigation

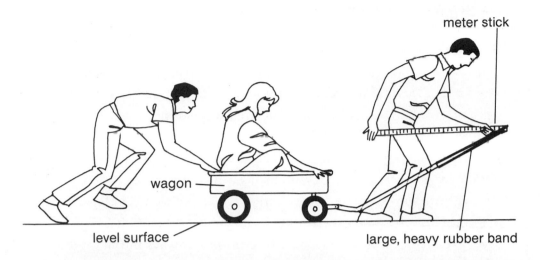

FIGURE 2-1 *When you apply a steady force to a wagon, what happens to its speed?*

2-1. He found that when a constant force acts on an object, the object's speed increases. Its speed does *not* remain constant, as Aristotle said it would.

When the speed of an object changes with time, we say that the object *accelerates*. Since speed is measured in terms of distance per unit time (distance/time, or distance ÷ time), such as miles per hour or kilometers per hour, acceleration is measured by finding how fast speed changes. For example, we can measure acceleration by finding how much the speed changes in one second—that is, in miles per hour per second (mi/h/s), or kilometers per hour per second (km/h/s). For an object to accelerate twice as fast, its speed must change twice as much in each second as it did before.

Consider the example of a car moving at a constant speed of 30 km/h. If someone pushes down on the accelerator pedal of the car, the car's speed increases. It accelerates. If during each second that the driver "steps on the gas" the car's speed changes by 5 km/h (from 30 to 35 km/h in the first second, from 35 to 40 km/h in the next second), then the acceleration is 5 km/h per second. To double the car's acceleration, the driver would have to make its speed change by 10 km/h each second. Thus, after one second, a car that had been moving 30 km/h would be moving 40 km/h. How fast would it be moving after two seconds?

If you pull forward on a wagon, the wagon's speed increases. The wagon accelerates forward. However, if you pull backward on a wagon that is moving forward, the wagon's speed decreases. We say the wagon *decelerates*. The same thing happens to a car when the driver pushes on the brake pedal. We can think of this reduction in speed, or deceleration, as a negative acceleration— an acceleration opposite to the direction of motion. The speed becomes less. It's like subtracting speed; hence, the word "negative." In all cases, however, the acceleration is always in the same direction as the force that is being applied.

Newton found that when he doubled the force on an object, the object's acceleration doubled. When he tripled the force, the acceleration tripled, and so on. In the last investigation, you didn't have the equipment needed to actually measure the acceleration. If you had, you would have found the same results that Newton did, provided you took friction into account.

An accelerometer is a device that indicates when there is an acceleration. It also shows the direction of the acceleration. In the following investigation, you will build and test at least one accelerometer.

▲▲▲▲▲▲▲▲▲▲▲
INVESTIGATION 2–2: ACCELEROMETERS

Materials needed: clear plastic jar with screw-on cap · tape · thread · T-pin · cork or piece of Styrofoam or other light material · wire · water · small piece of soap · clear plastic vial or pill bottle and cap

Figure 2–2a contains the plans for a cork accelerometer built from a plastic jar and cap.

First build the cap assembly. If the cap has no cardboard liner, refer to 1 in the figure: Tape one end of a piece of the thread to the inside of the cap and use the T-pin to attach the other end to the cork or piece of Styrofoam or other light material. If the cap has a cardboard liner, refer to 2 in the figure: Attach a short piece of the wire to the cardboard liner as shown. With the T-pin, attach one end of the thread to the wire and the other end of the thread to the cork or piece of Styrofoam or other light material.

Fill the plastic jar (shown in 3 of Figure 2–2*a*) with water and screw on the cap assembly. Figure 2–2*b* shows the finished cork accelerometer.

A second accelerometer that you can build is shown in Figure 2–2*c*. Fill the vial or plastic pill bottle with water. Leave a small space at the top so a small bubble will be inside the vial after the

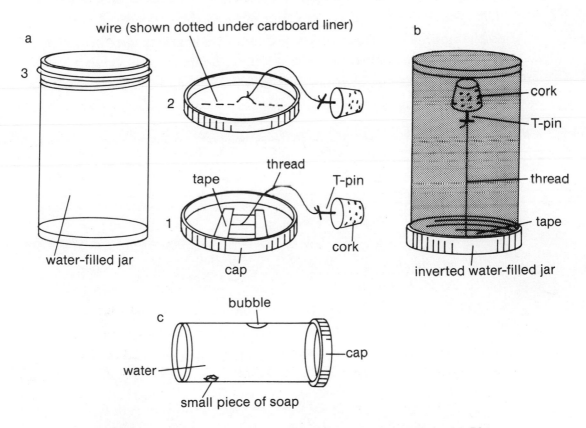

FIGURE 2-2 *An accelerometer is used to measure acceleration. (a) Plans and materials for a cork accelerometer. (b) The assembled cork accelerometer. (c) A bubble accelerometer.*

cap is put on. Add the small piece of soap to prevent the bubble from sticking to the sides of the vial. Cap the vial and turn it onto its side.

Place either or both of these accelerometers on a table or counter. Push the accelerometer to the left so that it accelerates to the left. Which way does the cork or bubble move while the jar or vial is accelerating to the left? Which way does the cork or bubble move when the jar or vial is slowing down? In this case, acceleration is to the right (or is negative, which is to say the same thing.) The force is also to the right. As you can see, the cork or bubble moves in the direction of the acceleration or force.

Repeat the experiment you did during Investigation 2-1, with an accelerometer in the wagon or mounted on the toy vehicle or roller skate. Does the bubble or cork move in the direction of the acceleration? Does the accelerometer indicate anything about the size of the force applied to the object being pulled?

Carry an accelerometer in a level position as you walk. Do you accelerate when you walk?

Going in Circles

It may surprise you to learn that sometimes we accelerate even when we travel at a constant speed. Suppose you are riding on a merry-go-round. You are moving in a circle at constant speed. But, according to the first law of motion, you should move *in a straight line at constant speed unless something pushes on you.* Since you're actually moving along a curved path, rather than in a straight line, there must be a force pushing you inward toward the center of the merry-go-round. This force pushes you off the straight-line path you would otherwise follow. If there's a force, there must be an acceleration. You are therefore accelerating. Acceleration is present when there is a change in direction as well as when there is a change in speed.

You'll find out more about what happens when things move along a curved path when you do Investigation 2-3.

▲▲▲▲▲▲▲▲▲▲▲
INVESTIGATION 2–3: ROUND 'N' ROUND WE GO

Materials needed: plastic pail · water · cork accelerometer · tape · bubble accelerometer · turntable or Lazy Susan · clay · marble · clear plastic cake dish or similar container

When an object moves in a circle, an inward force keeps it moving along the circular path. To feel that inward force for yourself, partially fill a plastic pail with water. Hold the handle of the pail in both hands as you turn around, swinging the pail in a horizontal circle. You can feel the inward force your arms must exert on the pail to keep it from flying off. This inward force that keeps a body moving in a circle is called a *centripetal force.*

Since the force is toward the center of the circle, we'd expect the acceleration to be in the same direction. To see that there really is an inward acceleration, try this. Hold the cork accelerometer at arm's length and turn around several times. **Don't turn so long that you get dizzy!** What is the direction of the acceleration as indicated by the accelerometer?

To see this in another way, tape the bubble accelerometer to a turntable or Lazy Susan along a radius as shown in Figure 2–3. You may need to put some clay under the accelerometer to make it level. What is the direction of the acceleration when the turntable moves? Can the bubble accelerometer detect a change in the size of the acceleration when the turntable rotates at different rates? Does the acceleration get bigger or smaller when the speed of the turntable increases?

To see what happens when the centripetal force on an object that is moving in a circle is removed, try the following experiment. Place the marble on a smooth surface. Place the clear plastic cake dish or similar container over the marble. Set the marble in motion along the inside edge of the cake cover or similar round container. You can do this by moving the container in small circles. Once you have the marble going in a circle, stop

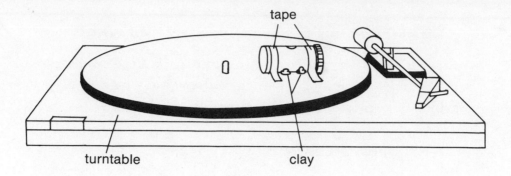

tape

turntable   clay

FIGURE 2-3 *Can you detect any acceleration if you tape a bubble accelerometer to a spinning turntable?*

moving the container. Let the marble slow down to a speed that you can easily follow with your eye. If you now tip the container so that the marble can escape from one side, which of the paths shown in Figure 2–4 do you think the marble will follow? Which path does it follow? Can you explain why it takes the path it does? (Don't forget the first law of motion!)

▲▲▲▲▲▲▲▲▲▲▲
EXPLORING ON YOUR OWN

▼If you've ever ridden a loop-the-loop roller coaster, you know that when you're upside down in the loop, you don't fall from the seat. You can see this same effect with a plastic pail that contains about a half-liter (a pint) of water. Hold the pail in your hand with your arm at your side as you normally would. You'll find that you can swing the pail in a vertical loop, like a roller coaster car, and the water won't fall out. That is, as long as the pail is moving along a circular path when it is upside down, the water will stay in the pail. For this to be true, how must the acceleration of the pail toward the center of the circle compare with the acceleration due to gravity?

▼Color Plate I shows people in a spinning "barrel." As you can see, they appear to be stuck against the wall. Can you explain what makes them "stick"?

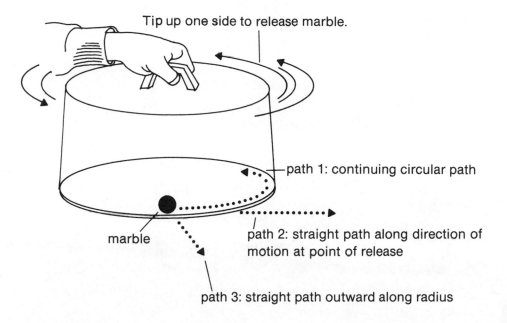

Tip up one side to release marble.

path 1: continuing circular path

marble

path 2: straight path along direction of motion at point of release

path 3: straight path outward along radius

FIGURE 2-4 *Which path will the marble follow when the centripetal force is removed?*

▼Can an accelerometer detect a difference in the acceleration at points near and far from the center of a spinning turntable? Design an experiment to find out. What do you find? Can you explain your results?

▼At what point on a turntable is the speed zero? Do you think the acceleration at this point is zero? Design an experiment using your accelerometer to find out. How is the speed of a point along the radius of a turntable related to the inward acceleration at that point?

▼Take your accelerometer with you when you travel on a bus, car, train, or airplane. Does your accelerometer detect the accelerations of the vehicle in which you are traveling? What does the accelerometer tell you about the direction of the force and acceleration when you go around a curve?

▼Take your accelerometer for a ride on a merry-go-round. Can it detect an inward acceleration from your seat on the merry-go-round? In which of the seats on the merry-go-round would you expect to find the largest acceleration? The smallest? Test your predictions at these positions. Were you right?

JUST FOR FUN

▼Fill a narrow-necked plastic bottle, such as a one-liter soda bottle, with water. Notice how it gurgles when you turn it over and let the water run out. Now move the bottle in small, fast circles as the water empties. Notice how the water swirls, creating a whirlpool, or *vortex*.

▼Ride a loop-the-loop roller coaster. You'll find there's a force on your bottom even when you're upside down at the top of the loop.

▼At the Franklin Institute Museum of Science, you can take a ride in the spinning chair shown in Color Plate II. You'll enjoy seeing what happens to your spin speed when you move the weights inward and outward.

Force, Acceleration, and Amount of Matter

Suppose you change the amount of matter in the object you pull. If you replace a 50-pound person in your wagon with a 100-pound person and apply the same force, will the acceleration be the same? (If you're using the smaller version of the experiment, you might place two weights on the toy vehicle instead of one.) What do you think will happen to the acceleration when you try to pull more matter with the same force? Try Investigation 2–4 to see whether you're right.

▲▲▲▲▲▲▲▲▲▲▲
INVESTIGATION 2–4:
ACCELERATION AND THE AMOUNT OF MATTER

Materials needed: materials used in Investigation 2–1

Pull the same wagon that you used in Investigation 2–1, using the same force. Have your friend seated in the wagon hold an accelerometer in a level position as you apply the force. Next, apply the *same* force with *two* people in the wagon. How does the acceleration of the wagon with two people on board compare with the acceleration with just one person? What does the accelerometer indicate about the acceleration when the number of people in the wagon increases? (If you used the mini-version of this experiment, do the experiment again with an accelerometer taped to the small toy vehicle or roller skate. Then repeat the experiment, using about twice as much matter as before, and apply the same force.)

Newton, Mass, Weight, and Motion

Newton realized that the amount of matter in an object would affect its acceleration. He called the amount of matter *mass*.

Newton found that if the force remains the same, the acceleration halves when the mass doubles. When the mass triples, the acceleration becomes one-third as big. This should not surprise you. If you apply the same force to a bowling ball and to a baseball, you know that the baseball will speed up much faster than the bowling ball.

What you call weight is related to mass, but is really a measure of the force exerted by gravity. Newton knew that the amount of matter in an object, its *mass,* which is measured in kilograms (kg), does not change with location. The *weight* of an object, which is measured in pounds or newtons (N), does depend on location. Suppose you rode a spaceship to Mars. Your mass would not change because you would contain the same amount of matter on Mars that you did on Earth, (assuming you didn't go on a diet or get sick along the way). You could measure your weight on Mars with a spring scale just as you do on Earth when you stand on a bathroom scale. The earth's gravity pulls you downward, causing you to compress the spring. On Mars, standing on the same scales, you would find you weigh *less*.

Gravity on Mars isn't as strong as it is on Earth. The same would be true on the moon, but near the giant planet Jupiter you would weigh much more. The weight of a 100-lb. person on the moon and on the planets is given in Table 2–1 in both pounds (lb.) and newtons (N). The person's mass would be 45 kilograms (kg) everywhere.

TABLE 2–1. *Weight of 100-lb. person on the moon and planets. Note that the person's mass remains constant.*

Location	Weight (lb.)	Weight (N)	Mass (kg)
Earth	100	441	45
Moon	16	71	45
Mars	38	168	45
Mercury	36	159	45
Jupiter	254	1120	45
Saturn	105	463	45
Venus	88	388	45
Uranus	103	454	45
Neptune	140	617	45
Pluto	45	198	45

The Second Law of Motion

Your investigations in this chapter have probably led you to the following conclusions:

1. When a force acts on an object, the object accelerates.
2. If the force is doubled, the acceleration doubles.
3. If the mass is doubled, the acceleration is halved (assuming that the force remains the same).

Together, these conclusions constitute the *second law of motion*. This is another law developed by Newton. His first law of motion described what happens when a force is not acting: a body maintains its state of motion (that is, motion or rest). The second law tells us what happens when a force *is* applied. The law states that force is equal to mass times acceleration. Thus, if the mass is constant, the acceleration increases when the force increases. If the mass increases and the force stays the same, the acceleration decreases.

Newton recognized that a force is needed to produce an acceleration. He also realized that an acceleration need not involve a change in speed. As you saw during Investigation 2-3, a centripetal force is needed to make an object move in a circle at constant speed. An accelerometer reveals that there is an inward acceleration when an object moves along a circular path. In this case, the force makes the object change its direction but not its speed. An acceleration can involve a change in direction, a change in speed, or both. In all cases, however, an object accelerates only while a force is acting on it. If the force is removed, the first law of motion comes into play. You saw this when you released the marble that was moving in a circle in Investigation 2-3. When there was no force pushing the marble inward, it moved at constant speed in a straight line along the direction in which it was moving at the moment it was released.

Now it's time to move on to explore another aspect of motion. In the next chapter, you'll have a chance to explore Newton's third law of motion, which applies to forces and motions of objects that are acting on one another. Taken together, Newton's three laws provide a basis for explaining any motion in the universe.

▼▼▼▼▼▼▼▼▼▼
CHAPTER

3

▲▲▲▲▲▲▲▲▲▲

YOU PUSH ME, I PUSH YOU

Suppose you push against a building or a big tree. Why doesn't it move when you push on it? Such objects are firmly attached to the earth. When you try to move one, it's really almost as if you are trying to move the earth. The earth is huge (its mass is about 6,000,000,000,000,000,000,000,000 kg), so any acceleration it might acquire from your push is too small to be measured or noticed. If you tried to push a building or a tree while standing on ice or loose sand, you'd find that you accelerate away from the object. This means that the earth is pushing you in a direction opposite to the direction that you are pushing. To see whether this is always true, try the activities in Investigation 3-1. They will allow you to see what happens when two objects push or pull on one another.

▲▲▲▲▲▲▲▲▲▲▲

INVESTIGATION 3–1: PUSH AND BE PUSHED, PULL AND BE PULLED

Materials needed: two spring scales · two skateboards or wagons, or two small carts with roller-skate (or similar) wheels · 10 ft. (3 cm) of clothesline · rubber bands: one strong, one long, several regular · tape · spring-type clothespin or short, stiff spring · two toy trucks or cars · string · block of clay or stone · three regular marbles or one large and two regular marbles · soda straws · scissors · stick or pencil

Test the two spring scales to make sure they read very nearly the same when the same mass is hung from each of them. Connect the two scales as shown in Figure 3-1. Have a partner hold one scale in a fixed position while you pull on the other. How hard does the spring scale show that you are pulling on your partner? How hard is your partner pulling on you? If you increase the force with which you pull, does your friend automatically increase his or her pull, too?

Connect the springs and attach one spring to a wall, a fence, a closed door, or some other large object firmly fixed to the earth. Pull on the earth through the two springs. How does the force you exert on the earth compare with the force the earth exerts on you?

For the next part of the investigation, sit on one of the skateboards, wagons, or carts that is resting on a flat, smooth, level surface away from other objects. Have a partner sit on the other vehicle facing away from you, as shown in Figure 3-2.

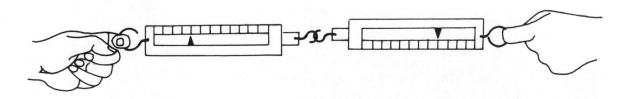

FIGURE 3-1 *How do the two forces compare when two people pull on each other?*

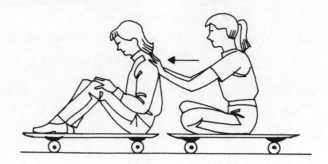

FIGURE 3-2 *If I push you, do you automatically push me?*

Reach out and push on your partner's back. What happens? Which way did you move? Which way did your partner move? When you pushed your partner, did he or she automatically push you?

Now turn things around. Let your partner push against your back. What happens this time? Did you automatically push your partner?

Try the same experiment on someone considerably heavier than you. How does your speed immediately after the push compare with the speed of your heavier partner? Next, repeat the experiment with someone who has less mass than you do. What happens this time? Which of you is moving faster immediately after the push?

Now see what happens when the force is a pull rather than a push. Attach one end of a length of the clothesline to the skateboard, wagon, or cart on which your partner is seated. While seated in the second vehicle, pull on the other end of the clothesline, as shown in Figure 3-3. In which direction do you move? In which direction does your partner move? Are you pulling on your partner's vehicle? How do you know that your partner's vehicle is pulling you?

Repeat the experiment, but this time pull against a wall or a fence. Do you move? Which way do you move? Does the wall move?

Which way do you move if you *push* on the wall or fence?

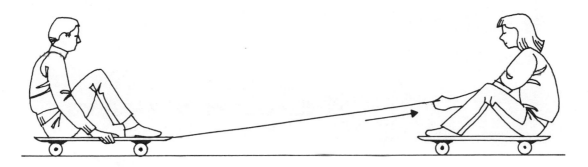

FIGURE 3-3 *If I pull on you, do you automatically pull on me?*

Next, use a piece of the tape or the wide, thick, strong rubber band to attach the spring-type clothespin or short, stiff spring to one of the toy cars or trucks, as shown in Figure 3–4. If you use a clothespin, tie its handles together with string so the jaws are wide open, as shown in the drawing. Place the second toy car or truck against the other side of the spring. Work on a nonflammable surface far from any flammable object. **Ask an adult to burn the string with a match** so that the spring will suddenly "explode," allowing the toy vehicles to push on each other through the exploding clothespin. (Of course, you could compress the spring by pushing the toy vehicles together instead of tying the clothespin handles together. However, it's very difficult to release both vehicles at the same time. By having an adult burn the string, you can be sure that the force will act on both vehicles at the same time. If you can't find an adult to help you, snip the string with scissors.)

What happens when the spring is released? We'll call the toy vehicle to which you attached the clothespin vehicle A, and the other one vehicle B. Did vehicle A push on vehicle B? How do you know that vehicle B pushed back on vehicle A? How did their speeds compare after the spring had been released?

Add the block of clay or stone to one of the toy vehicles to make it more massive than the other. Repeat the experiment. Which vehicle moves faster immediately after the spring "explodes"?

Remove the clay or stone and connect the two toy vehicles with

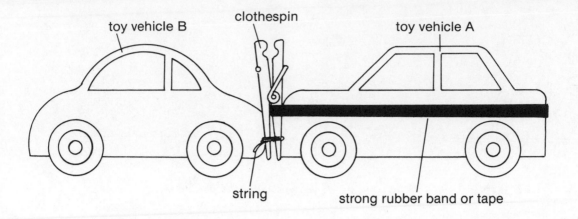

FIGURE 3-4 *What happens when one toy car or truck pushes on another?*

the long rubber band. Pull the two vehicles apart so the rubber band is stretched a small amount. Can you feel vehicle A pulling on vehicle B? Can you feel vehicle B pulling on vehicle A? What happens if you release the two vehicles at the same time? Does vehicle A pull on vehicle B? Does vehicle B pull on vehicle A?

Add the block of clay or a stone to one toy vehicle to make it more massive than the other toy vehicle. Repeat the experiment. Which vehicle moves faster immediately after they are released?

Now use a rubber band to connect one of the toy vehicles to a fence, a wall, a concrete block, or some other very heavy object. Pull the vehicle away from the heavy object so as to stretch the rubber band a little. What happens when you release the vehicle? Does the vehicle move? Does the heavy object move?

Finally, place one of the toy vehicles with an attached spring next to a wall. When you push the vehicle firmly against the wall, you compress the spring. Release the vehicle. Which way does it move? Does the wall move?

In the final part of the investigation, tape a marble to each of two soda straws, as shown in Figure 3–5. Use the scissors to notch one end of each soda straw, as shown in the same drawing. Connect the notched ends of the straws with a regular rubber band. Move the straws apart so as to stretch the rubber band.

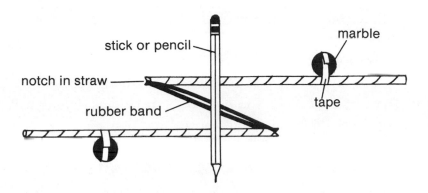

FIGURE 3-5 *What happens when one marble pushes on another through a rubber band?*

Place the straws, marbles, and stretched rubber band on a smooth table or floor. Place the stick or pencil on the straws to hold them in place. Then suddenly lift the stick to release the straws. Which way do the marbles (and straws) move? How do their speeds compare immediately after they are released?

Repeat the experiment, but this time tape a large marble or two regular ones to one straw and a single regular marble to the other. Which way do the marbles move when the straws are released? How does the speed of the heavy marble compare with the speed of the lighter marble?

▲▲▲▲▲▲▲▲▲▲▲
EXPLORING ON YOUR OWN

▼While sitting still on a swing, hold onto one of the swing ropes with one hand. Use the other hand to hold a heavy ball. Give the ball a hard push to toss it toward a friend who is standing in front of you. Which way do you move after throwing the ball? Can you explain why?

▲▲▲▲▲▲▲▲▲▲▲
JUST FOR FUN

▼The next time you go ice skating or roller skating, ask a friend to stand in front of you with his or her back to you. Push against your friend's back. This is similar to what you did in the second part of Investigation 3–1, except this time you and your friend will be standing on skates. You'll see that both you and your friend move apart when you push on him or her. If you do the pushing, he or she automatically pushes back on you.

Newton's Third Law of Motion

Color Plate III shows a tennis racquet hitting a ball. The racquet exerts a force on the ball and changes the ball's direction. If you look closely, you can see that the ball is also exerting a force on the racquet. Notice how the strings of the racquet are stretched by the collision with the ball.

Newton was the first to notice that if you push someone or something in one direction, that person or thing will automatically push you in the opposite direction. Furthermore, the push that you receive has exactly the same strength as the push you give. These observations constitute the *third law of motion:* for every action (force), there is an equal and opposite reaction (force).

It is important to note that the two forces act on *different* objects. When you push *on the floor,* simply by standing on it, the floor pushes back *on you* with an equal force in the opposite direction. The force of gravity is the force that is pulling you downward and causing you to push against the floor. This force can also cause you to move. If you jump from a chair, the force of gravity will make you accelerate downward. When you reach the floor, the floor exerts a force against you and brings you to rest.

The force of the earth's gravity is what causes you to move downward. Do you exert an equal and opposite force on the earth while you are falling from the chair to the floor? The answer is yes! Why then do you not see the earth accelerating toward you as you accelerate toward it? The reason is that because the earth is so massive its acceleration toward you is much too small to detect.

Remember, the force that you exert on it is equal to the force it exerts on you. Its mass times its acceleration is equal to your mass times your acceleration. Since the earth's mass is about 100,000 billion billion times yours, its acceleration will be equal to yours (about 10 meters/second/second or 36 kilometers/hour/second) divided by 100,000 billion billion.

If you have ever tried to step from a small boat onto a dock, you know that the boat moved backward. (See Figure 3–6.) You may even have landed in the water if the boat wasn't tied closely and firmly to the dock. As you used the boat to push yourself forward, you were pushing backward against the boat with the same force that it was pushing you forward. This is yet another example of Newton's third law of motion applied in a real situation.

Investigation 3-2 will show you how the third law of motion is related to a very common action—walking.

FIGURE 3-6 *The third law of motion holds true when you try to step from a boat to a dock. The law is not all wet, but you may be if you're not careful!*

▲▲▲▲▲▲▲▲▲▲▲

INVESTIGATION 3–2:
MOVING ON THINGS SMALLER THAN EARTH

Materials needed: long, heavy plank or board · large dowels or metal rollers · toy electric or spring-powered train and sections of track or large battery-powered toy truck or car · long, narrow, thin board · small dowels or round pencils

Place the long, heavy plank or board on the wooden dowels or metal rollers spread out along a smooth, level floor, as shown in Figure 3–7. **With an adult to hold you on one side and a friend on the other, carefully step onto the plank.** Stand on the plank for a moment and, **while still holding onto your friend and an adult,** begin to walk. Which way do you move? Which way does the plank move?

Normally when you walk, you push backward against the earth. The earth, in turn, pushes you in the opposite direction and so you move forward. Because the earth is so big, you don't see it move when you push on it. But, when you try to walk on a plank, which probably has less mass than you do, you can see it

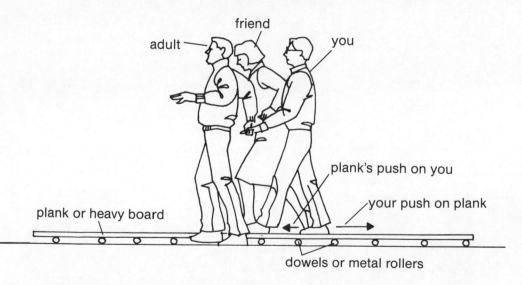

FIGURE 3-7 *If you walk this plank, you'll never go overboard.*

move when you push on it. Further, you can see that it moves in a direction that is opposite to the way you move. You push it in one direction and it pushes you in the opposite direction.

You can do a similar experiment on a smaller scale. Mount the toy electric or spring-powered train and a straight length of the track on the long, narrow, thin board. (You can substitute a large battery-powered toy truck or car on a similar board without the tracks.) Place the board on the small pieces of dowel or round pencils. Start the train moving in one direction along the track. See whether you can predict the direction that the track and board will move.

Momentum and the Third Law of Motion

In the investigation you just completed, you may have observed what happens when two objects pushing on each other have different masses. The heavier object seems to move slower than the lighter object after they push on each other. You saw the same effect during Investigation 3–1: after two masses pushed on each other, the bigger mass always had a smaller velocity than the smaller mass.

The mass of an object multiplied by its velocity is called the *momentum* of the object. Experiments conducted by Newton and others have shown that the changes in the momentum of two objects that push on each other will always be equal and in opposite directions. [Another way of expressing this is to say that the total momentum is conserved (unchanged).] Suppose a 2-kg mass and a 1-kg mass are at rest and are attached by a compressed spring that is then released. If the 2-kg mass moves away with a velocity of 10 mi/h, the 1-kg mass will move in the opposite direction at 20 mi/h.

When you walk, the situation is more complicated. You acquire momentum in one direction, but you don't see anything with an equal momentum moving in the opposite direction. The reason is that it is the earth that you are pushing on when you walk. The earth's mass is so great that the tiny velocity it acquires is far too small to be noticed. It's similar to trying to see the earth's acceleration when you jump from a chair.

▲▲▲▲▲▲▲▲▲▲▲
INVESTIGATION 3–3: BALLOON ROCKETS AND MOMENTUM

Materials needed: skateboard or small cart mounted on roller-skate wheels · heavy ball (for example, a medicine ball) or pillow · balloon · tie bands or twist ties · soda straw · sticky tape · toy truck or car with wheels that turn freely · thread

When a rocket or jet plane moves, it doesn't have to push against the earth. It pushes gases produced by burning fuel at very high speed out the rear nozzle of the rocket. The moving gas, in turn, pushes the rocket forward. In this investigation, you'll have an opportunity to build one or more simple rockets of your own.

Sit on the skateboard or small cart mounted on roller-skate wheels while holding the heavy ball or pillow. Hold the ball or pillow next to your chest with both hands. Then push it away from you and the cart with as much force as you can muster. (Be sure you don't throw it at something that can break.) How are you like a rocket? Since the momentum you acquired is the same as the momentum of the ball you threw, why do you move so slowly?

For the next part of the investigation, blow up the balloon and seal its neck with a tie band (twist tie). Attach the balloon to the soda straw with sticky tape as shown in Figure 3–8. Run one end of a long piece of the thread through the straw. Tie one end of the thread to a hook or some firmly anchored object near the ceiling. You can hold the other end of the thread on the opposite side of the room, with the balloon near your end. Have a partner hold the neck of the balloon and remove the tie band. Then watch the balloon "blast off" when your partner lets go.

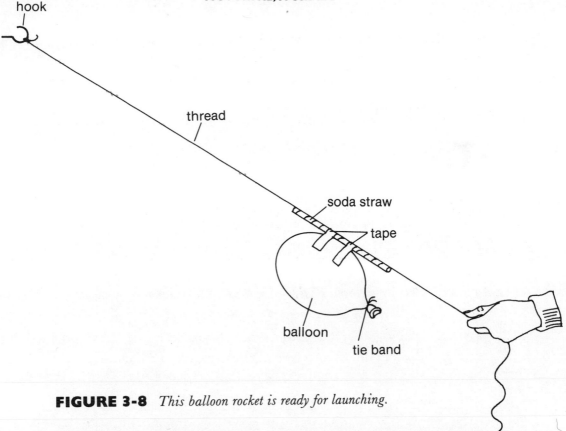

hook

thread

soda straw

tape

balloon

tie band

FIGURE 3-8 *This balloon rocket is ready for launching.*

What is the balloon rocket's "fuel"? Why does the balloon move so much faster than you did when you threw a heavy ball from a cart?

To do the final part of the investigation, blow up a balloon, seal the neck with a tie band, and tape the balloon to the body of the toy truck or car. Place the truck on a smooth, level surface. Hold the balloon's neck as you remove the tie band. Then release the neck of the balloon, so the air inside can "blast out." What happens to the toy truck or car? Why does the vehicle move so much more slowly than the thread-mounted balloon did earlier?

▲▲▲▲▲▲▲▲▲▲

EXPLORING ON YOUR OWN

▼Cut away one side of an empty cardboard milk carton. Float the boatlike remainder of the carton in a sink or bathtub that is partially filled with water. Cut a small hole above water level in the middle of the stern (rear end) of your boat. Place the balloon in the boat and run its neck through the small hole you made. The hole should be small enough to hold the neck of the balloon firmly in place. Blow up the balloon. When you release the neck of the balloon so air can escape, you'll have a balloon-powered rocket boat.

See whether you can predict what will happen to the boat's speed if you place some "cargo" in the boat, reinflate the balloon, and again let the balloon rocket provide power to the boat. What happens to the boat's speed as you continue to add cargo to it? Explain.

▼Build a balloon rocket and a sailboat mounted on balsa wood, like the ones shown in Figure 3–9. (As you can see, you may be able to modify the air car you built for Investigation 1–1 to make this rocket.) Mount the rocket on the balsa-wood platform that rests on small wooden dowels or round pencils. What happens when you let air escape from the balloon?

Next, place the sailboat on the balsa-wood platform, and hold the balloon rocket in your hand so that it cannot move. Let the air emerging from the firmly held balloon push on the sail of the sailboat. What happens to the sailboat in this "wind"?

Now place both the balloon rocket and the sailboat on the balsa-wood platform, which should be resting on the dowels. Arrange them so that the air coming from the balloon rocket pushes on the sail. Why is there no motion when the sailboat and rocket are arranged this way? Finally, what will happen if you remove the balsa-wood platform and repeat the last experiment with both the balloon rocket and the sail on the rollers?

▼An object moving with a certain velocity has a momentum. Unless a force acts on the object, it will maintain its momentum. An object moving in a circle has momentum, too, but the direction of its motion is continually changing. Such an object is said to have *angular momentum*. Like ordinary momentum, angular momentum also is conserved (unchanged).

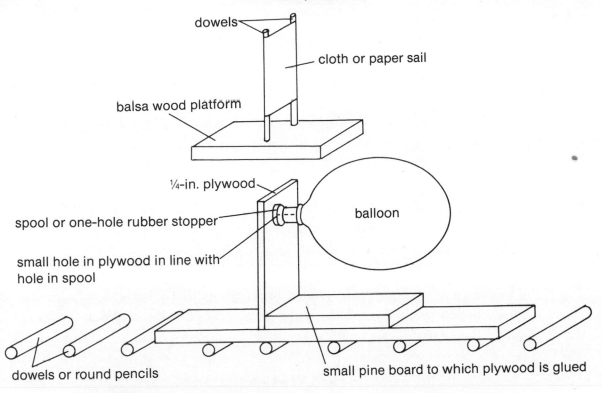

dowels

cloth or paper sail

balsa wood platform

¼-in. plywood

spool or one-hole rubber stopper

balloon

small hole in plywood in line with hole in spool

dowels or round pencils

small pine board to which plywood is glued

FIGURE 3-9 *What do you think will happen when the balloon rocket shoots its "exhaust" at the sailboat?*

In the case of angular momentum, the product of mass, velocity, *and radius* (distance from the center of the circular motion) is maintained, rather than just mass times velocity. To see that this is true, sit in a swivel chair and hold a dumbbell or a heavy weight in each hand. **Be sure the chair is sturdy and that you can turn in it safely.** Hold the weights close to your chest, and have someone give you a push so that you are spinning around in the chair. Now slowly move your arms outward. What happens to your speed of rotation as you increase the radius of the path of the weights?

Now bring the weights back to your chest. What happens to your rotation speed now? Repeat this experiment several times to see what happens as you increase and decrease the radius of the circular path of the weights.

At the Franklin Institute Science Museum (and probably at

some other science museums), there is a spinning chair with movable masses that was mentioned in Chapter 2. The masses are conveniently arranged so that you can easily increase and decrease the radius of the circular path through which they move. You can change your speed of rotation dramatically by moving the masses in and out from the center of the rotation. (See Color Plate II.)

▼Angular momentum can be used to distinguish an uncooked egg from a hard-boiled egg. To see how, obtain an egg of each kind. Place one of the eggs on a table and spin the egg. While it is spinning, stop it and then quickly let go. Repeat the experiment, using the other egg. How can you tell which egg was hard-boiled? To test your answer, break open and eat the egg that you think is hard-boiled. Unless you like raw eggs, you'd better think about your choice before cracking the shell!

▲▲▲▲▲▲▲▲▲▲▲
JUST FOR FUN

▼You can become a rocket on skates. The next time you go ice skating or roller skating, take along a medicine ball or a heavy pillow. Stand on your skates at rest, holding the medicine ball or pillow. Then, with your knees bent, push the ball or pillow away from your body with both hands. You'll find yourself moving in the opposite direction, like a rocket that has fired some fuel.

In this chapter, you have investigated some of the relationships among force, motion, and momentum. In the next chapter, you'll investigate more closely a force that's been with you all your life. It's one that none of us can avoid—the force of gravity.

▲▲▲▲▲▲▲▲▲▲

GRAVITY: A FORCE THAT'S USUALLY WITH US

Not every force makes something move. You can push on a house all day and it won't move. The entire weight of a house pushes down on the foundation, but the house does not move downward. That's because the foundation provides an equal upward push that keeps the house in place. If the house or a part of it could be raised off the foundation and then released, it would go crashing down. It would fall because the earth would pull on it. The earth exerts a similar force on buildings, cars, trucks, elephants, mice, the moon, satellites, and even you.

We call the force that the earth exerts on everything around it *gravity*. No one knows *why* gravity exists, but it does. Physicists believe that there are only four basic types of force in the universe and that gravity is one of them. The other three are the electromagnetic force, the strong nuclear force, and the weak nuclear force.

The electromagnetic force results from tiny particles that have what is called electric charge. This force is actually the one that acts when we observe ordinary pushes and pulls. For example, the ordinary muscular forces that we use to overcome gravity or push on things may seem to arise simply because of contact. In fact, contact involves electrical forces between objects. When the molecules of one object get very close to those of another object, an electrical repulsion sets in that tends to push the objects apart. It is this repulsion that allows us to push things. Friction is another example of a force that results from the electrical forces between particles of matter.

What about magnetic forces? you might ask. Magnets seem able to pull on things almost as if by magic. Actually, magnetic forces arise because of electric forces within the matter that makes up a magnet.

The final two types of forces—the strong and the weak nuclear forces—arise deep within *atoms,* the building blocks of matter. Atoms have a center called a *nucleus.* The particles within the nucleus produce forces that are different from the electromagnetic forces.

Feeling Forces on a Bicycle Ride

The next time you ride your bike, stop to think about what you feel as you ride. At first, you have to push very hard on the pedals. Then, as your speed increases, you find it easier and easier to push these same pedals. Finally, when you reach your cruising speed, it's quite easy to keep the bike moving at the same rate—until you come to a hill, that is. Then the forces you have to apply become larger as you go up the hill. You may shift to a lower gear or get off and walk. On the other hand, if you're going down the hill, you don't even have to pedal to keep moving.

At the beginning of your bike trip, a big force is needed to make the bike and your body accelerate. Remember, you found that the bigger the mass is, the bigger is the force needed to make the mass accelerate. When you start out, you have to apply a force that accelerates your entire body as well as the bike, and that amounts to a fair amount of mass. If you want to reach cruising speed very quickly, that will require an even bigger force because a larger acceleration requires a larger force. As you approach cruising speed, the acceleration decreases and so does the force needed. That's because, as you may recall, the smaller the acceleration is for a given mass, the smaller is the force needed. Finally, at cruising speed, there is no acceleration. The speed of the bike is constant. Ideally, you would not have to apply any force to keep going. However, there is a frictional force that keeps acting. It arises because the road pushes against the tires, and it tends to make the bike decelerate. There is also a backward force due to air resistance. As you ride through the air, you have to push the air out of the way. The air pushes back on you with an equal force. In Color Plate IV you can see how a cyclist tries to reduce air resistance by pushing against less air. You have to apply a "forward" force equal and opposite to the "backward" force of friction that opposes your motion.

As you know, your bike will coast quite far on a smooth, level road. On such a road, the force of friction is not very big. That's why the force you have to apply to the pedals is quite small once you get your bike up to cruising speed.

When you come to an uphill stretch of road, part of the force of gravity tends to pull you and your bike back down the incline. To overcome that force, you have to apply a force in the other direction. That force comes from your feet pushing on the pedals. On the other hand, when you are going downhill, part of the force of gravity pulls you and your bike in the direction you're traveling. Therefore, you can stop pedaling if you want to: gravity will probably provide all the force you need to move down the hill. If the force of gravity along the incline just equals the force of friction between the tires and the road, you'll coast down at a steady speed. If the force of gravity acting down the hill is greater than the force of friction, you'll accelerate.

Mass and Weight on Earth

In Table 2–1 on page 36, you found how your weight would vary from planet to planet. The force of gravity depends on the mass of the planet. The more massive the planet is, the greater in general is its pull on other objects. However, the force also depends on the distance from the center of the planet. Jupiter's mass is actually 318 times as great as the mass of the earth. Yet, as you see in Table 2–1, you would not weigh 318 times as much on Jupiter as you do on Earth, but only about 2½ times as much. The reason is that the radius of Jupiter is more than 11 times the radius of the earth. Standing on its surface would put you a long way from its center. And every time the distance between the centers of two masses is doubled, the force of gravity is reduced to a quarter of its former strength. Although some people can jump high on the earth (Color Plate V), jumping is easier on the moon (Color Plate VI) because the force of gravity on the moon is about one-sixth that on the earth.

To see how the earth's force of gravity is related to the mass on which it pulls, you can carry out Investigation 4–1.

▲▲▲▲▲▲▲▲▲▲▲

INVESTIGATION 4–1: GRAVITY AND MASS

Materials needed: masking tape · set of standard masses or some identical large washers · spring scale, preferably one that measures forces in units of newtons

As you know, a spring scale can be used to measure force. With such a scale, you can measure the force that gravity exerts on different masses. The scale you use should be calibrated in the standard force units called newtons. If your spring is calibrated in grams or kilograms instead, you can easily recalibrate it. Simply cover one side of the scale with a piece of masking tape. If it is calibrated in grams, then, at the mark corresponding to 100g (g is the abbreviation for grams), write *1N* (1 newton). Similarly, write

2N at the 200-g line, *3N* at the 300-g line, and so on. If the spring is calibrated in kilograms, write *10N* at the 1-kg line (kg is the abbreviation for kilogram), *20N* at the 2-kg line, and so on. (This works fairly well because, on the surface of the earth, mass in kilograms × 9.8, or nearly 10, equals the force or weight in newtons.)

Hang a 100-g mass on the spring scale. With what force, in newtons, does the earth pull downward on a 100-g mass? On a 200-g mass? A 500-g mass?

If you don't have a set of standard masses, use large, identical washers. To be sure they are identical, weigh each one separately. Then find the weight, in newtons, of one, two, three, and more washers.

If possible, compare your results with those of others who have done the same experiment. Do your data agree with theirs? What happens to the force that the earth exerts on a mass when the mass doubles? If the mass is tripled, does the force of gravity triple, too?

Making a Prediction About the Way Falling Objects Accelerate

The results of Investigation 4–1 probably did not surprise you. You know that bigger masses are harder to lift. The earth seems to pull harder on big masses than on small ones. However, the fact that doubling an object's mass doubles the force of the earth's gravity on it should enable you to make a prediction about the acceleration of falling objects.

You know that a given mass will accelerate twice as fast when the force on it is twice as great, since force = mass × acceleration. You also know that if one mass is twice as big as a second mass, then twice as much force will be needed to give the second mass the same acceleration as the first. Now suppose you have objects of two different masses—let's say a baseball and a golf ball. See whether you can predict how the downward accelerations of the baseball and golf ball will compare. Then test your prediction in Investigation 4–2.

▲▲▲▲▲▲▲▲▲▲▲
INVESTIGATION 4–2: ACCELERATION DUE TO GRAVITY AND AIR RESISTANCE

Materials needed: tennis ball, baseball, golf ball, lacrosse ball, or others with different masses · sheets of paper · balance

To test the prediction you have made, choose two balls that have different masses. Whatever masses you choose, hold both of them so that their lowest points are at the same height above the floor. Then release them at the same time. It's not easy to release two objects at the same instant, so you'll probably want to practice first, and then repeat this experiment several times.

What do you conclude about the time it takes both masses to fall to the floor from the same height? What do you conclude about the acceleration of these two masses when pulled by the earth? Do your results agree with the prediction you made?

Now try dropping a ball at the same time you drop one of the sheets of paper. Why do you think the ball has a greater acceleration than the paper?

Before you repeat the experiment, squeeze the paper into a tight ball. How do you think the acceleration of the two objects will compare now? Try dropping them. Were you right?

Why does the paper fall faster when it is squeezed into the shape of a ball? Its mass hasn't changed. (If you think it has, try weighing a few of the sheets of paper on the balance. Then squeeze them into a ball and weigh them again.) One possibility is that air resists the movement of the paper just as water resists a swimmer. Perhaps the surface area (length ✕ width) of the paper in contact with the air affects the force of air resistance. To check out this idea, fold a sheet of the paper in half. In this way, you halve the area of the paper exposed to the air. Try dropping a piece of this folded paper at the same time you drop an identical piece that has not been folded. Does the surface area affect the rate of fall of the paper?

▼Does a falling object really accelerate? Is its speed over the second meter (or yard) that it falls greater than its speed over the first meter (or yard)? To find out, hold a stone or a ball about 1 m (or 1 yd.) above the ground or floor. At the moment you drop the object, start counting, "one, two, three, four...," as fast as you can, to time its fall. (Most people can get to "five" in just about a second.) Repeat this several times until you get consistent results for the approximate time of fall.

Now that you know the approximate time for the ball or stone to fall 1 m, measure the time it takes the object to fall 2 m. Does it take twice as long? If it doesn't take twice as long, what does this tell you is happening to the object's speed as it falls?

▼Hold a book flat and place a sheet of paper on the book's top cover. Be sure the paper does not stick out beyond the cover of the book. If it does, trim the paper to make it smaller. Now drop the book. Do book and paper fall together? Or does the paper fall more slowly? How can you explain your results?

▼Tape a paper clip to a handkerchief or sheet of paper, as shown in Figure 4-1. The cloth or paper will serve as a parachute for the paper clip. Now at the same instant drop the paper clip that is attached to the parachute and an unattached paper clip. Observe the rate at which each falls.

Terminal Velocity

You've seen that an open sheet of paper falls more slowly than one

tape on underside of cloth or paper

cloth or paper

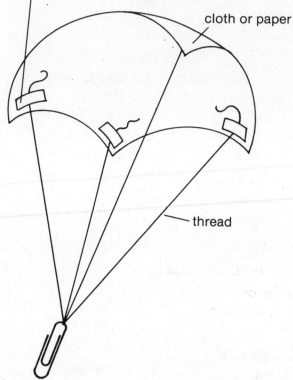

thread

FIGURE 4-1 *A handkerchief or piece of paper could serve as a parachute for a paper clip.*

that has been crunched into a small ball. The open sheet of paper falls much like a leaf from a tree. As a leaf or a sheet of paper falls, air pushes upward on the paper, opposing the force of gravity that is pulling the object downward. Of course, air pushes against a falling ball, too. However, the surface area of the bottom of a typical ball is much smaller than the surface area of a typical sheet of paper. Furthermore, the ball is much heavier than the paper. Consequently, the force of air resistance on a ball is only a small fraction of its weight (the downward pull that the earth exerts on it). In the case of a sheet of paper, the upward force of air resistance may be as large as the weight of the paper. If it is, the paper will not accelerate.

Divers, like the one shown in Color Plate VII, reduce splashing by minimizing the surface area that first touches the water. At the same time, they reduce the air resistance as they fall. By assuming a "spread eagle" posture, the skydiver seen in Color Plate VIII provides a *large* surface area. This increases the force of air resistance, as you found during Investigation 4–2. From riding your bike at various speeds, you know that air resistance also increases with speed. After a few seconds, the air resistance acting upward on the skydiver equals the diver's weight. When the two forces are equal, the net force on the diver is zero. With zero force, there is no acceleration, and the skydiver falls with a constant speed. This speed is called the *terminal velocity*. Objects falling through air will eventually reach a terminal velocity. In the case of light objects with a large surface, such as leaves or feathers, the terminal velocity is small and is reached very quickly. In the case of a steel ball, the terminal velocity is much larger and is reached only after the ball has fallen for a few seconds.

In a vacuum tube—a tube from which all the air has been removed—all objects fall with the same acceleration because there is no air resistance. In such a vacuum, a coin and a feather, or a steel ball and a leaf fall side by side.

Air Pressure and Barometers

If you've ever pumped air into a bicycle tire or blown air into a balloon, you know that the air in the tire or balloon pushes back against you. The air inside pushes against the surface of the tire or the balloon. The force that it exerts per area of surface is called *pressure*. In this case, since the pressure is due to air, it's called *air pressure*. If you put more air into the tire, the pressure will get bigger because there will be more air to push against the same surface of the tire. That is, force per unit area will increase.

The earth pulls on everything, including the air, which covers it like a huge, invisible sea. Consequently, air has weight. We live at the bottom of this sea of air, which pushes on us just as water does when we swim beneath the surface of a sea, lake, pond, or pool. The total weight of the air is enormous. It all pushes on the air at the earth's surface, so the air we live in is under pressure. We can measure this pressure with a barometer, like the one shown in Figure 4–2. In a mercury barometer, the space above the mercury is a vacuum; it contains no air or other gases.

The push of the air on the surface of the mercury in the dish is transferred upward to the mercury column as well. This is because pressure in a fluid is equal in all directions. At sea level, the pressure of the air balances a mercury column about 76 cm (30 in.) tall. If we know that the bottom of the tube has an area of, say, 1 square centimeter, we can find the air pressure. We also need to know that the weight of this column of mercury is just about 10 N. This means that a force of 10 N pushes down on the 1 square centimeter of surface at the bottom of the column. If we express the force in pounds and the area in square inches, the pressure is 14.7 pounds per square inch. That means that in order to balance this mercury column the air must exert an equal pressure: 14.7 pounds per square inch.

The pressure of the air varies from place to place and from day to day. On a mountain top, the pressure is less than at sea level because the column of air above a mountain is shorter than the column above an ocean. Rainy weather is usually associated with low-pressure air, so a falling barometer often indicates the approach of foul weather.

We often use air pressure to push matter from place to place. Sometimes, a pump compresses air in a tank and the resulting pressure is used to move liquid through pipes. In Figure 4–3a, you see how compressed air is used to lift a car. Sometimes, a vacuum or partial vacuum is created by removing air from a vessel. Outside air pressure can then push matter toward the vacuum. A syringe like the one shown in Figure 4–3b operates on this principle. When the piston is pulled up, it reduces the pressure of the gas inside the syringe. As a result, the outside air pressure pushes liquid up into the cylinder of the syringe.

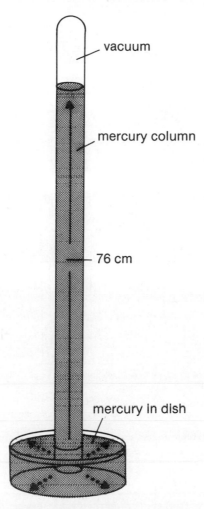

vacuum

mercury column

76 cm

mercury in dish

The pressure (force per area)
is equal in all directions.

FIGURE 4-2 *A mercury barometer can be used to measure air pressure.*

In the next investigation, you'll examine the pressure at different depths and directions in a liquid and see how air pressure can support a column of water.

▲▲▲▲▲▲▲▲▲▲▲

INVESTIGATION 4–3: PRESSURE, WATER, AND AIR

Materials needed: hammer · small nail · tall metal can · mask-

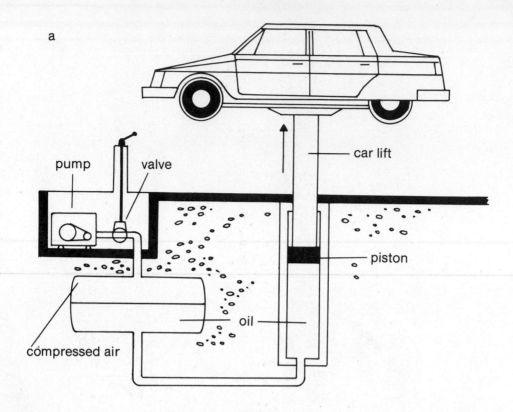

a

pump   valve   car lift

                                  piston

compressed air   oil

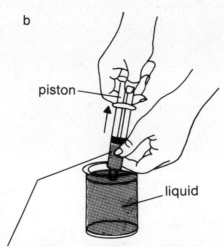

b

piston

liquid

The pressure is reduced here when the piston
is pulled out.

FIGURE 4-3 *Using air pressure to do useful work. (a) Compressed air is used to lift a car. (b) Air pressure pushes a liquid into a syringe when the pressure inside the syringe is reduced.*

PLATE I *The people in this amusement park ride are held against the inside wall of the ride by friction caused by a centripetal force.*

PLATE II *From the blur in the photographs, you can tell that the boy moves faster when he pulls the weights in (top) than when he leaves them extended (bottom).*

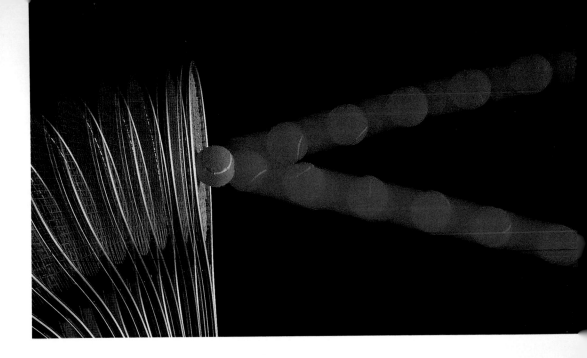

PLATE III *When you hit a tennis ball, you apply a force to the ball. Does the ball exert a force on you?*

PLATE IV

Why do you think this cyclist is bent over so far?

PLATE V *People can jump high on the earth but not as high as they could on the moon.*

PLATE VI *The force of gravity is less on the moon than on the earth, so this astronaut can jump much higher there than anyone can jump on earth— and with less effort, too.*

PLATE VII *Divers minimize their surface area before entering the water to minimize the splash.*

PLATE VIII   *Would this skydiver move faster in a cannonball position?*

PLATE IX *Levers come in various shapes and sizes. Which ones are you familiar with?*

PLATE X *Even a small child can lift 500 pounds if he or she uses this giant lever at the Franklin Institute Science Museum.*

ing tape · water · test tube or vial · paper towel · large glass tumbler · clear plastic soda straw or glass tube · food coloring

Use the hammer and small nail to punch several holes along a line running from the top to the bottom of the tall metal can. Then punch several holes around the base of the can at the same height as the bottom hole you made before. Figure 4–4 shows the can with the holes. Cover the holes with tape and fill the can with water. Hold the can over a sink and have a partner remove the tape. How can you tell that the water pressure is greater near the bottom of the can than near the top? How can you tell that the pressure is equal in all sideways directions at the same height?

To see how air pressure can support a column of liquid, fill the test tube or vial to the brim with water. Then lay a small piece of the paper towel over the mouth of the tube so that it covers the opening. Carefully turn the tube or vial upside down. You'll find

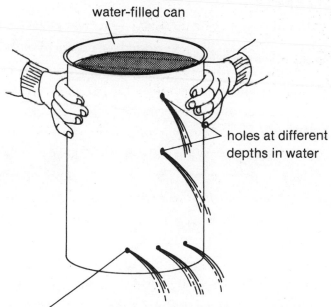

water-filled can

holes at different depths in water

holes that allow water to flow out in different directions at same depth

FIGURE 4-4 *You can use a can like this one to see the effect of depth and direction on water pressure.*

that the water will remain in the vessel without any support from you. Air pressure will hold the paper against the tube and keep the water from falling out.

Place the inverted tube in the large glass tumbler about three-fourths full. Pull the paper away from the mouth of the tube, which should be below the water surface. Slowly lift the vessel until its mouth is just below the level of the water in the glass. Then very slowly tip up one side of the tube. You'll see bubbles of air entering the tube to replace the water. What pushes them up the tube?

Once the tube is filled with air, move it slowly down into the water. Why doesn't water refill the tube or vial? Figure out a way to fill the tube with water while it is submerged in the glass tumbler, and do it.

When the container is nearly filled with water, slowly lift it, but keep its mouth below the surface of the water. What keeps the water in the tube?

Lower one end of the clear plastic soda straw or glass tube into a glass of water to which you have added a drop or two of the food coloring. How high does the water rise inside the straw? Wet your finger and place it over the top of the straw, as shown in Figure 4–5. Slowly raise the straw. Where is the water level in the straw now? Keeping your finger over the upper end of the straw, lift the straw from the container. What do you think keeps the water in the straw? How must the pressure at the bottom of the water column in the straw compare with the pressure at the top of the water column? What happens when you lift your finger from the top of the straw?

Repeat the experiment, but this time see whether you can release a single drop of water by carefully lifting your wet finger just a little bit. Once you've mastered the technique of releasing single drops of water, see whether you can figure out why your method works. The device you have made is called a *pipette*. Chemists use pipettes to transfer small, measured volumes of various liquids.

straw or glass tube

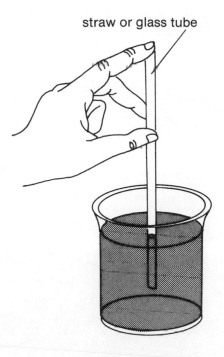

FIGURE 4-5 *Can you lift water in the straw or glass tube by placing your finger over one end in the manner shown?*

▲▲▲▲▲▲▲▲▲▲▲
EXPLORING ON YOUR OWN

▼Find an aneroid barometer—the kind normally found hanging on walls in homes. Take the barometer to a tall building. Read and record the pressure on the ground floor of the building. Then carry the barometer to the top floor and again record the pressure. How can you account for the change in pressure? Can you detect the pressure difference between the lower and upper floors of a house? Take your barometer along when you ride in a car. Can you detect changes in pressure when you go up and down hill? When you climb a mountain?

▼To see the effect of area on pressure, place several dowels with different diameters on soft clay, as shown in Figure 4–6. Have a friend support one of the dowels while you place a pile of books on its top surface. Let the dowel sink into the clay as far as it will go.

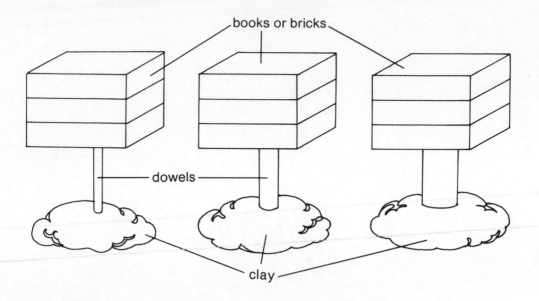

FIGURE 4-6 *What happens to the pressure when the same force pushes on different areas?*

Then remove the books and the dowel. You'll see the impression that the dowel made in the clay. Now repeat the procedure, using the same pile of books on each of the dowels you have. When you have finished, compare the depths of the impressions made by the different dowels. Under which dowel was the pressure greatest? Under which dowel was the pressure smallest?

▼A siphon is a device that is often used to move water or other liquids from one place to another. It is based on the difference in air pressure at the two ends of a tube filled with the liquid being transferred. To see how a siphon works, you'll need two large containers and a length of rubber or plastic tubing. As an alternative, you can use two flexible straws. Put the end of one straw into the other and seal the junction with masking tape. Fill one container with water and place it on a counter next to a sink. Place the other container in the sink. Use a length of tubing that will reach from one container to the other. To fill the tubing with water, lower it gradually into the container of water. Coil the tube around the bottom of the container as you go. When the tube is filled, hold your finger over the upper end of the tube, lift that end, and put it on the bottom of the empty container in the sink. Keep the other end in the water-filled upper container. (See Figure 4–7a.) What happens when you remove your finger?

Another way to fill the tube is to hold it in a U-shape under a running faucet. When it is full, put a finger over both ends of the tube. Put one end into the water-filled upper container. Put the other end into the lower, empty container. Then remove your fingers from the ends of the tube. What happens?

After about half the water has flowed from the upper container to the lower one, have a partner hold the tube while you raise the lower container. Raise the container until the end of the tube in your container is higher than the end that is in the other container. What happens to the direction of the water flow when you reach this point? What can you do to change back the direction of the water flow to the way it was?

Figure 4–7b shows two setups for "siphon races." In one, the heights of the two water-filled containers are different. In the other, the diameters of the tubes are different. Can you predict the winners in each race? Try to design some siphon races of your own.

▼Find a wide-mouthed bottle and a cork or rubber stopper that fits the mouth of the bottle. Fill the bottle almost to the top with water. Leave a small air space at the top. Add enough water to an eyedropper so that when it is placed in the bottle it just barely floats in a vertical position. Only the tip of the rubber bulb should be above the water. Put the cork or rubber stopper into the mouth of the bottle. Push down gently on the cork or stopper so as to increase the pressure of the small amount of air at the top of the bottle. What happens to the eyedropper? Can you make the eyedropper rise again? Can you make the eyedropper float in the middle of the bottle like a submarine? How do you explain the up-and-down motion of the eyedropper?

▼Calculate the total force with which the air would push on your body if you were at the beach by the ocean on a clear day.

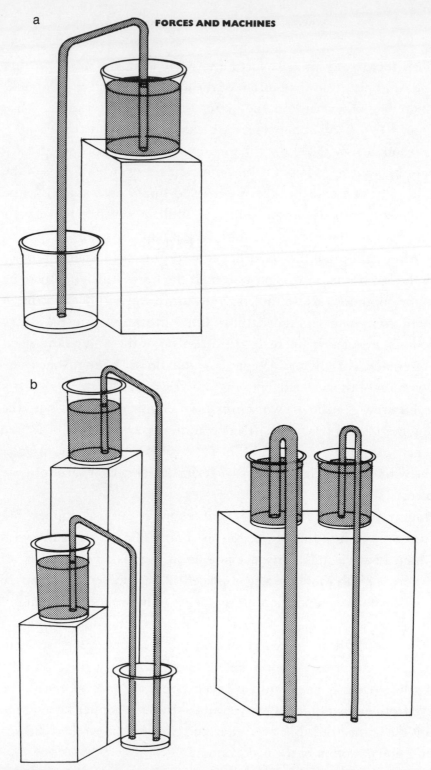

FIGURE 4-7 *Experiments with siphons. (a) A simple siphon. (b) Two setups for siphon races. Which siphon will win in each case?*

▲▲▲▲▲▲▲▲▲▲▲
JUST FOR FUN

▼ Use a pin to punch a few holes about 2 in. (5 cm) from each end of a soda straw. Give a friend or a member of your family a cool drink. Then offer him or her the straw with the holes. See whether the person can figure out why it's impossible to drink from the straw.

Center of Mass

When you carry a long object such as a board, you probably hold it in the middle so it won't rotate or turn. Similarly, if you want to carry a tray full of dishes with one hand, you put your hand under the center of the tray rather than near its edge. The point on an object at which you can support it so that it doesn't rotate is called the *center of mass*. It's the point in the object where you can consider all its mass to be located. If you lift or support something at its center of mass, it feels as if all the object's weight is at that point.

In the next investigation, you'll find the center of mass of an object. You'll also make some predictions about where to lift an object so that it will balance and not rotate.

▲▲▲▲▲▲▲▲▲▲▲
INVESTIGATION 4–4: CENTER OF MASS

Materials needed: scissors · large sheet of cardboard · pin · washers or other small weights · string · pencil · meter stick or yardstick · rectangular block

Use the scissors to cut an irregular shape like the one shown in Figure 4–8a from the large sheet of cardboard. Pin the cardboard to a bulletin board or a post in such a way that the sheet can turn freely. From the same pin, suspend some of the washers or other small weights on the end of the string, as shown in Figure 4–8b. Since the weight will be pulled by gravity, it will pull the string downward in a straight vertical direction. Once the weight is at rest, use the pencil to draw a line along the string near the center of the cardboard. Then pin the cardboard from a different corner, as shown in Figure 4-8c. Make another line along the string that crosses the first line you made. Do this one more time and make a third line. The point where all three lines meet should be the center of mass.

To see whether the point you found is in fact the center of mass, remove the irregular-shaped cardboard from its point of attachment and try to support it on your finger at the point you marked. If the cardboard is balanced and doesn't rotate, the point is the one where all the mass can be considered to be located. If you can't support the cardboard at this point, repeat the experiment, being careful to draw the lines exactly along the string.

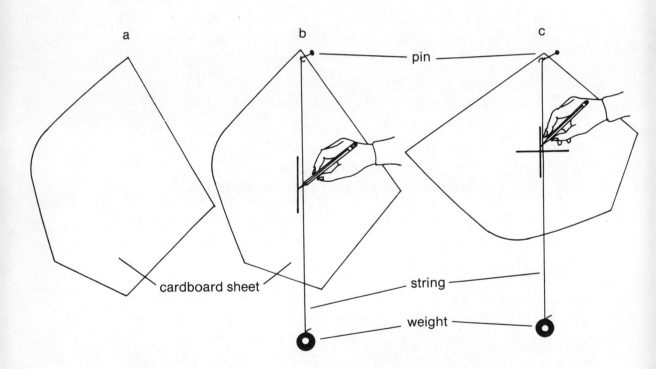

FIGURE 4-8 *With a weight, string, pencil and a pin you can find the center of mass of a flat object.*

Where would you expect the center of mass of the meter stick or yardstick to be? Test your prediction by seeing whether the stick will balance at the point you selected. Where would you expect the center of mass of a square sheet of cardboard to be located? How can you check your prediction?

Stand the rectangular block on one end. Make a mark on the side of the block that you think is in line with the center of mass (Figure 4-9a). Tip the block just a bit to one side so that the center of mass is still directly above part of the base (Figure 4-9b). Let go of the block. Notice that it swings back to its original position. What happens if you tip the block so that the center of mass is beyond the base of the block (Figure 4-9c)? Can you explain why?

To see what happens when your own center of mass gets beyond the base that your feet provide, try this. Stand perpendicular to a wall so that your right shoulder and right foot are against the wall. Where is your center of mass? Try to lift your left foot. What happens?

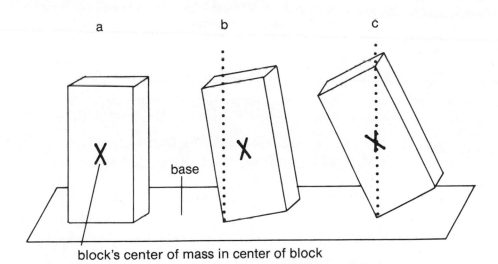

FIGURE 4-9 *What happens when the center of mass moves? (a) A block's center of mass is at the center of the block. (b) A tipped block whose center of mass is still above part of the block's base. (c) What happens when the block's center of mass is beyond its base?*

▲▲▲▲▲▲▲▲▲▲▲
EXPLORING ON YOUR OWN

▼Where would you expect the center of mass of a cube to be located? How about that of a ball? How about that of a hollow ball, such as a tennis ball? Your intuition probably tells you that the center of mass of a hollow ball should be at the very center of the ball, even though there is really no mass there. In this case, your intuition is right.

To see a case in which the center of mass is at a place where there is no mass, try this. Find the center of mass of a dinner fork by balancing it on your finger. Then insert a quarter, a half dollar, or a large washer between its two upper tines. Attach a second fork in the same way (see Figure 4–10a).

Where do you think the center of mass of the two forks is? You should be able to balance the forks by placing the coin on a capped soda bottle. Can you balance the forks with the coin through their two lowest tines? Explain your results.

▲▲▲▲▲▲▲▲▲▲▲
JUST FOR FUN

▼Figure 4–10b–d shows some other "balancing acts" in which the center of mass lies in space. See whether you can duplicate them, and then invent some mysterious balancing acts of your own.

Tensile Strength: Another Kind of Pressure

A suspension bridge hangs from large cables. To be certain that these cables will not break, engineers have to know the tensile strength of the metals found in these cables. Tensile strength is a measure of how much force per unit area can be applied to an object without stretching it or pulling it apart. Tensile strength thus measures the *pull* per unit area that something can withstand. (Air pressure, you may recall, measures the *push* per unit

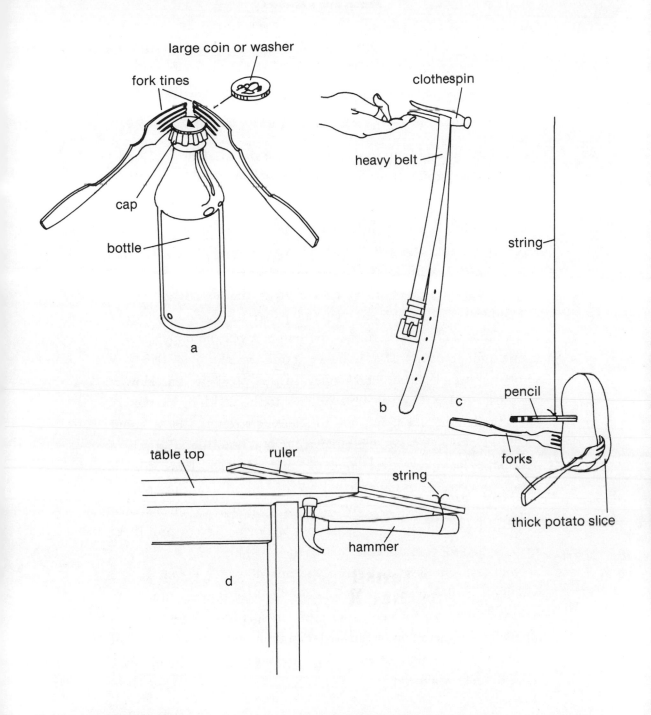

FIGURE 4-10 *An object's center of mass need not be within the object. (a) The center of mass of a pair of forks and a coin. (b-d) Some other balancing acts.*

area on a surface.) In the next investigation, you'll measure the tensile strength of paper.

▲▲▲▲▲▲▲▲▲▲▲

INVESTIGATION 4–5: THE TENSILE STRENGTH OF PAPER

Materials needed: scissors · plain white paper (8 ½ × 11 in.) · ruler · newspaper · samples of different brands of paper towels · wrapping paper · tape · pliers · paper clip · spring scale

Use the scissors to cut the sheet of plain white paper crosswise into a number of strips 8 ½ in. long. Vary the width of the strips from about ⅛ in. to 1 in., using the ruler to do the measuring. Then cut about ten ¾ in.-wide strips from another sheet.

Hold one of the narrow strips of paper as shown in Figure 4–11a, and pull. Be careful not to bend or twist the paper as you try to pull it apart. If you have trouble breaking a strip, ask someone to pull on one end while you pull on the other. How is the tensile strength of the paper related to the width of the paper? Does the length of a strip seem to affect its strength? How about the kind of paper? For example, find out how the strength of newspaper compares with that of writing paper. How does it compare with that of paper towels? With that of wrapping paper?

Using the ¾-in. strips, cut some patterns like the ones shown in Figure 4–11b, as well as some of your own. Try to pull these strips apart. Can you predict where they will break?

Now test samples of different brands of paper towels to see which one is the strongest. You'll need the tape, pliers, equal-size strips of the paper towels, paper clip and spring scale—as well as a partner—to help you. Each strip can then be tested as shown in Figure 4–11c. Which paper towel is the strongest? Which one is the strongest when wet?

▲▲▲▲▲▲▲▲▲▲▲

EXPLORING ON YOUR OWN

▼Some bridges and other heavy structures rest on columns. In

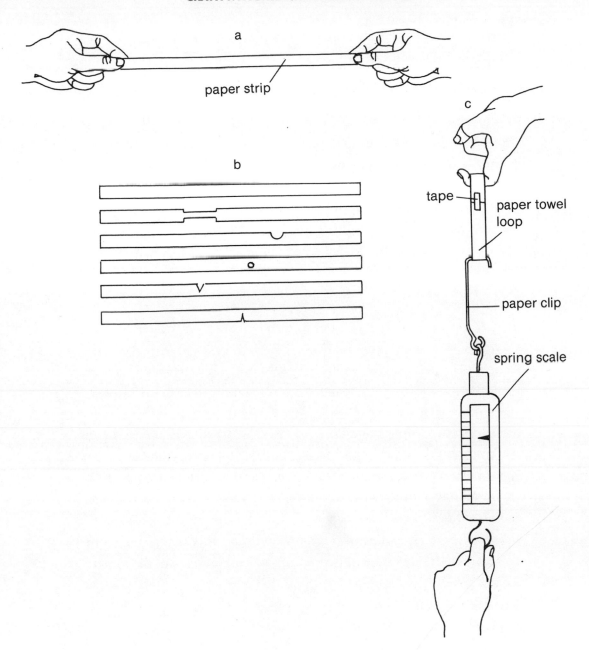

FIGURE 4-11 *Setups for testing the strength of paper.*

such structures, what's important is compression strength, or the ability of the columns to resist being compressed. To test the compression strength of a sheet of paper, roll it into a tube, secure the middle with a piece of tape, and stand it upright on a bathroom scale. Push down on the paper column with a hard-cover book. How hard do you have to press before the paper column crumples and gives way?

Test a variety of papers in this way. Which one is the strongest? Is a narrow tube stronger than a wide one? How does the strength of a square-shaped column compare with that of a round one? With that of a triangular one? Is a column made from two sheets stronger than a column that is one sheet thick? Cut a column in half. How does the strength of the half-column compare with that of the original full-length column?

In this chapter, you've looked into some of the principles of gravitational attraction and observed some of the effects of gravity. In the next chapter, you'll look at another force that's always with us. It's a force that allows us to walk, to ride a bike, to open cans, to hold a glass, and to do most of the everyday tasks we perform. Yet the same force reduces the efficiency of most machines and hinders our rate of travel. This force is one that has already been mentioned several times in this book. It is called friction. Friction is one of the most common forces we know, but it's also one that is generally among the least understood.

▼▼▼▼▼▼▼▼▼▼

CHAPTER

5

▲▲▲▲▲▲▲▲▲▲

FRICTION: A FORCE THAT'S ALWAYS WITH US

What do you think is the most slippery surface there is? Do you think that slipperiness has anything to do with the object that's sliding over the surface? What does slipperiness have to do with friction? Is friction related to an object's weight or to its surface area? Do like surfaces stick together more than ones that are not alike? These are some of the questions you'll investigate in this chapter as you try to find out more about friction.

It's the frictional force between our feet and the earth that enables us to walk or run. It's friction between the road and tires that enables the earth to push back on a car and allow it to move. It's also friction between a moving car and the air that opposes the car's motion. If you think about it, friction is a force that's vital to us. Even though it reduces the efficiency of vehicles, it also makes possible motion along and near the earth's surface. We simply couldn't get along without friction.

There are various ways to measure the frictional forces between objects and the surfaces they slide on. Four methods are shown in Figure 5-1. When you do the next investigation, you can choose any one of these methods. They make use of small weights and a pulley, a sensitive spring scale, a long thin rubber band, or a board. If you follow the first method but don't have a set of standard weights (Figure 5-1*a*), you can use washers or paper clips instead. You can also use a smooth paper clip in place of a pulley. If you use the spring-scale method (Figure 5-1*b*), the scale must be a very sensitive one if you are using normal-size blocks; otherwise, you'll have to use large blocks. To use the rubber-band method (Figure 5-1*c*), you'll need a partner to hold a ruler and estimate the stretch of the rubber band. If you use the last method (Figure 5-1*d*), use a Masonite board to compare the slipperiness of different blocks. Measuring the height to which you have to raise one end of the board to make a block move is a simple way to compare friction for different blocks.

▲▲▲▲▲▲▲▲▲▲▲
INVESTIGATION 5–1: MEASURING FRICTIONAL FORCES

Materials needed: 4 to 6 smooth wood blocks of the same size (You may wish to ask an adult to cut them from a length of 2 in. × 2 in. lumber, and then you can smooth them with sandpaper.) · Method *a:* pulley or paper clip and thumbtack, thread, weights (or washers) · Method *b:* spring scale, tie band (twist tie) · Method *c:* thin rubber band, ruler · Method *d:* 18–24-inch-long, 8–12-in.-wide piece of ¼-in.-thick Masonite, smooth on one side · wide rubber bands · felt pads with sticky backing · thumbtacks · ruler or yardstick

Place one of the smooth wood blocks on a smooth, level surface. Use one of the methods illustrated in Figure 5-1 to measure the force needed to make it move at constant speed. When the block moves at a steady speed, there is no acceleration. Therefore, the

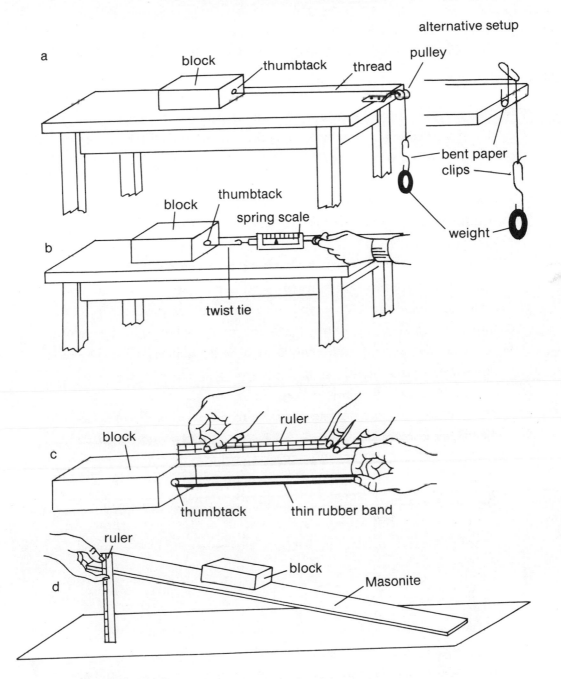

FIGURE 5-1 *Here are four ways to measure friction.*

pull on the block must be just equal to the force of friction, which is what you want to measure. If you use method *a* (weights and pulley), you will find the weight needed to make the block slide along at constant speed. If you use method *b* (spring scale), you can read the force on the spring scale. If you use method *c* (rubber band and ruler), you will need to find the length of the stretched rubber band. If you use method *d* (ruler and board), you'll find that you can measure friction by finding the height to which you have to raise the board to make the block slide. The height of the raised end of the Masonite board can be measured with a ruler or yardstick.

You will probably notice that it is easier to make the block slide once it gets started. It seems to stick more when it's at rest than when it's moving. To get rid of most of this "at-rest stickiness," tap the board or table on which the block rests as you slowly increase the force or raise the board. Make several trials to see how much your results vary. Once you've had a little practice, your results will probably become more consistent.

Now prepare some of the blocks with different surfaces to look like those shown in Figure 5–2: Leave one block unchanged (1). Put the wide rubber bands on a second block (2), the felt pads on a third (3), and the thumbtacks into another (4). The thumbtacks will go in easier if you use a second block to press on them (5). Now use one of the methods *a–d* described above and shown in Figure 5–1 to compare the friction between these blocks and the surface over which they slide. Which block is the most slippery? Which block is least slippery? Make a list of the surfaces in order of decreasing slipperiness.

Now try the same blocks on a surface other than the table top or Masonite board you have been using. You might use the rougher backside of a Masonite board, a piece of chipboard, a kitchen counter, linoleum, and so on. Does the surface on which the blocks slide affect the slipperiness? Does it affect the order of the blocks on your slipperiness list?

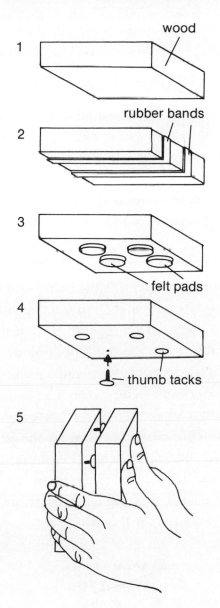

FIGURE 5-2 *The same block can have different kinds of surfaces.*

▲▲▲▲▲▲▲▲▲▲▲▲

EXPLORING ON YOUR OWN

▼Place the blocks used in Investigation 5–1 one after another in trainlike fashion on a smooth board. How can you arrange the blocks so that the "cars" in the train will stay together when you raise the board and make them slide down the hill? How can you arrange them so the cars in the train will all separate when you raise one end of the board?

▼Repeat the last part of Investigation 5-1. Try some other surfaces on your blocks, so that you can add to your "slipperiness list." You might try various kinds of coverings, such as writing paper, newspaper, aluminum foil, waxed paper, and plastic wrap. These can be taped onto the bottom of a block for comparison with blocks you've already tested. What other block surfaces can you test?

▼Place wide rubber bands on each of *two* blocks. Place both blocks on a Masonite board. Lift the board to be sure that both blocks begin to slide at about the same time. Now place a block with a thumbtack surface behind (on the uphill side of) one of the rubber-banded blocks. Do you think both blocks will slide at the same time now? Why or why not? Again, lift the board and test your prediction. Were you right?

▼Using the different surfaces you have tested and remembering what you learned about center of mass, try the following. Make a stack of four blocks that will slide together as a unit, one on top of the other, when you lift one end of the board on which the stack rests. Then make a stack that will fall over before the blocks slide when you raise one end of the board.

▲▲▲▲▲▲▲▲▲▲▲
JUST FOR FUN

▼Ask a pilot why jet airplanes fly at very high altitudes.
▼Which sneakers have the best grip? Does the pattern on the sole affect traction?

Weight and Surface

From experience, would you predict that weight affects friction?

For example, you may know that it's harder to push a loaded box along the floor than it is to push the same box when it's empty. In the next investigation, you'll explore the effects of weight and surface area on the force of friction.

▲▲▲▲▲▲▲▲▲▲▲
INVESTIGATION 5–2:
WEIGHT, SURFACE AREA, AND FRICTION

Materials needed: one of the four devices (*a–d*) used in Investigation 5–1 to measure friction · 3 or 4 identical plain wood blocks · thumbtacks · thread or tie band (twist tie)

Using one of the devices used in Investigation 5–1 to measure friction, find the force (or the amount of weight, or rubber-band stretch) needed to make one of the wood blocks move along a smooth, horizontal surface at a steady speed. Be sure to tap the surface so that the block doesn't have that extra "stick" that you found before.

Now place a second block on the first one. What have you done to the weight by adding another block? Again, measure the force (or related quantity) needed to make the blocks move at a steady speed. How does the force required to move a stack of two blocks compare with the force needed for a single block?

Try to predict how the force needed to pull a stack of three blocks will compare with the force needed to pull two blocks along the same surface. Then try it. Was your prediction correct?

To test the effect of surface area on friction, you must change the surface area without changing the weight. (Why must you keep the weight the same?) Can you think of a way to do this?

One way is to hook two blocks together like a "train" (see Figure 5–3): using (a) two tacks and thread or the tie band (twist tie) or (b) three thumbtacks. You already know the force needed to move the two blocks when they are stacked. Now you can keep the weight the same but change the area on which the friction

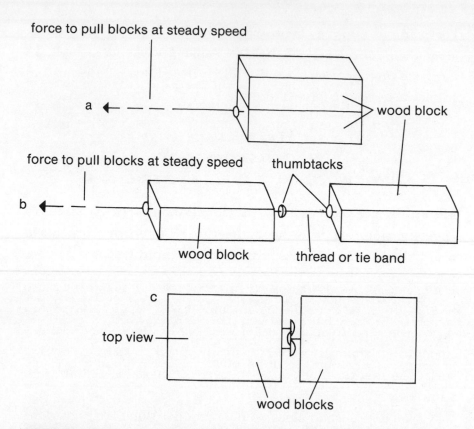

FIGURE 5-3 *You can change the surface area where friction occurs without changing the object's weight. How does the friction for (a) a stack of blocks compare with that for (b) a train of blocks?*

acts. What have you done to the total surface area in contact with the board or table by making the two blocks into a train?

Measure the force needed to move the two-block train at a steady speed. Do this several times. How does the force compare with the force needed to move a stack of two blocks with half the total surface-contact area? Repeat the experiment, using three blocks. How does the force needed to move a three-block train compare with the force needed to move a stack of three blocks?

If possible, compare your results with those of others who have done the same experiment. How do their data compare with yours? What can you conclude about the effect of weight on friction? About the effect of surface area on friction?

▲▲▲▲▲▲▲▲▲▲
EXPLORING ON YOUR OWN

▼How can you change the surface area in contact with a board or table if you use thumbtacks for the block's surface? Try doing so. Does doubling the thumbtack surface-contact area affect the force needed to overcome friction?

▼How can you change the surface area of contact for a rubber-band surface on a block? Does the amount of rubber surface affect the force needed to overcome friction?

▼Place a piece of paper on a smooth surface, such as a counter top. Try pushing and pulling the paper, using the nail sides of your fingers. Then try the same thing using your fingertips. Does it make a difference which side of your fingers you use? Does it make a difference how hard you push downward when you try to move the paper?

Try the same experiment on other surfaces, such as a carpet, slate, cloth, wood, and linoleum. Does the type of surface affect the ease with which you can move the paper?

Try different materials in place of the paper. You might use cardboard, plastic wrap, waxed paper, aluminum foil, newspaper, or other materials. Are some of them easier to move than others? Does it make a difference what surface they are on?

▼Rest the ends of a meter stick or yardstick on your hands as shown in Figure 5–4. Slowly slide your hands toward each other. At what point on the stick do they meet?

Next, start with one hand at one end of the stick and the other hand about a foot in from the other end. Where do you think your hands will meet this time when you slide them slowly together? Try it! Were you right?

Now let one end of the stick rest on a horizontal pencil that you hold in one hand. When you start to move the pencil and your other hand together, which one do you think the stick will begin to slide over first? Where do you think your hand and the pencil will meet?

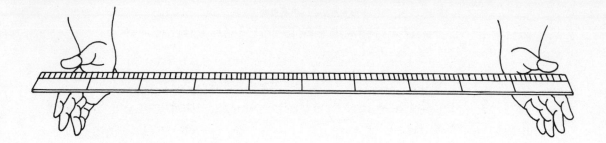

FIGURE 5-4 *Testing for friction using a yardstick or meter stick.*

Repeat the first part of the experiment with a large lump of clay near one end of the stick. Slowly slide your hands together. Where do they meet this time?

From what you know about friction and center of mass, try to explain the results of these experiments.

▲▲▲▲▲▲▲▲▲▲▲
JUST FOR FUN

▼At the Franklin Institute Science Museum, and perhaps at other science museums, too, you will find a simple device that demonstrates how friction varies with weight. The device consists of a stack of weights that have handles. You will find it more difficult to turn the weights near the bottom of the stack than the ones near the top.

▼See whether you can use friction to hang spoons from your nose, forehead, and cheekbones.

Friction and Wheels

We don't know who invented the wheel, but that invention certainly changed civilization forever. Just think of all the places where you find wheels and/or rollers. Don't forget the ones on the bottoms of kitchen or filing-cabinet drawers, bed frames, and refrigerator trays. In the next two investigations, you'll have a chance to explore the effect of wheels and rollers on friction.

▲▲▲▲▲▲▲▲▲▲▲
INVESTIGATION 5–3: FRICTION, ROLLERS, AND WHEELS ON A SMALL SCALE

Materials needed: one of the first three devices *(a–c)* used in Investigation 5–1 to measure friction · 3 or 4 of the plain wood blocks used in Investigation 5–2 · small dowels or round pencils · toy truck

Using one of the first three devices used in Investigation 5–1 to measure friction, measure the force needed to pull a stack of three or four blocks along a smooth, level surface. Then place the blocks on a series of the small dowels or round pencils and measure the force needed to make the blocks move along the rollers, as shown in Figure 5–5a. How does this "rolling friction" compare with "sliding friction," the kind you measured earlier?

Place the toy truck upside down on the stack of blocks you just used. Measure the force needed to overcome friction between the blocks and the surface (Figure 5–5b). Then place the blocks on the toy truck or car as shown in Figure 5–5c and measure the force needed to make the truck move. Notice that the total weight is the same in both cases. Do wheels reduce friction?

▲▲▲▲▲▲▲▲▲▲▲
INVESTIGATION 5–4: FRICTION, ROLLERS, AND WHEELS ON A LARGER SCALE

Materials needed: wagon · heavy-duty spring scale (optional) · sheet of cardboard big enough for someone to sit on · large dowels or metal rollers

Turn the wagon upside down and pull it to get a feel for the force needed to pull it along a floor or sidewalk as shown in Figure 5–6a. (If possible, use a heavy-duty spring scale to measure the force.) Then turn the wagon over so its wheels can roll, and pull it again. How does the force needed to roll the wagon at a steady speed compare with the force needed to drag it?

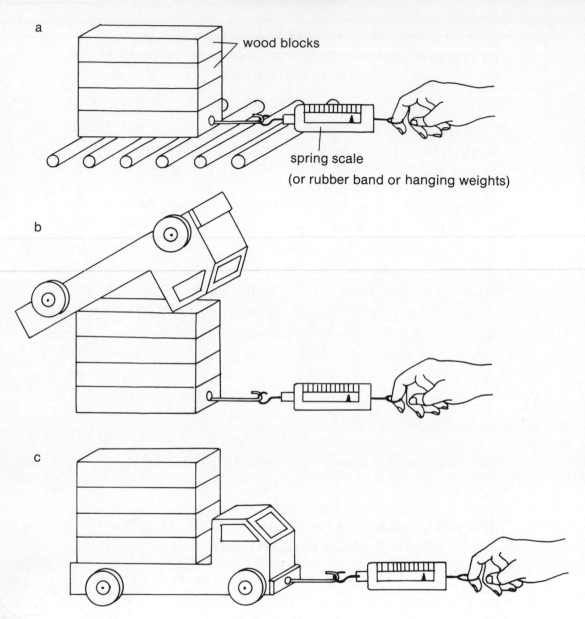

FIGURE 5-5 *Do rollers and wheels reduce friction?*

Have someone sit on the sheet of cardboard resting on the large dowels or metal rollers on the floor as shown in Figure 5-6*b*. Measure (or get a sense of) the force needed to pull the person along the surface. Now have the same person sit in a wagon, and measure the force needed to roll the wagon and passenger along at a steady speed. Can you predict how hard you'll have to pull to move the "wagon train" shown in Figure 5-6c? To move two people seated in the same wagon?

Now have a heavier person sit on the cardboard (see Figure

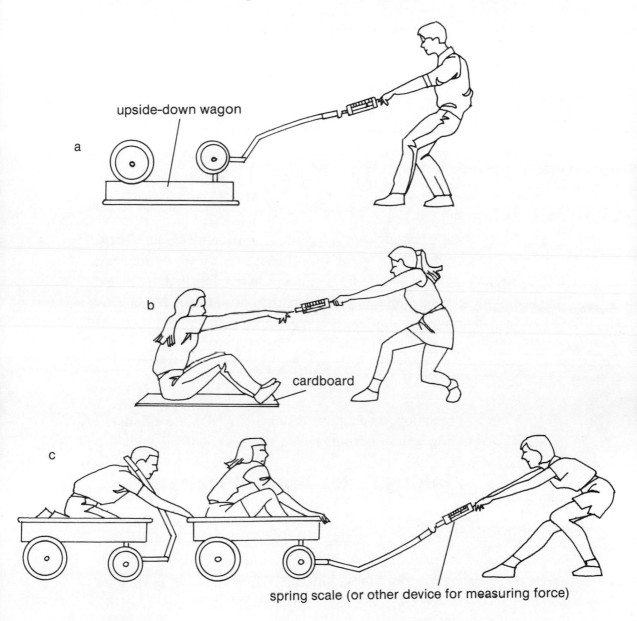

FIGURE 5-6 *Do larger wheels and rollers still help to reduce friction?*

5-6*b* again). Predict the force needed to move this person along at a steady speed. Have the same person sit on a sheet of cardboard that has twice the area as the first one. Predict the force needed to slide the person along at a steady speed now.

▲▲▲▲▲▲▲▲▲▲▲
EXPLORING ON YOUR OWN

▼Suppose you pull on a loaded wagon at different angles as shown in Figure 5–7. Does the angle at which you pull affect the force needed to make the wagon roll? Can you find an angle that makes it impossible to move the wagon forward no matter how hard you pull? Can you find an angle that makes the wagon move backward? If you run a rope through the wagon handle, can two people pull on the rope in different directions and still make it move straight ahead?

▼Place a large, sealed can of paint on an identical can. Notice how hard it is to turn the top can while it rests on the bottom can. Now lift the top can and put a number of marble "ball bearings" into the groove on the upper rim of the bottom can. Replace the top can and notice how easily it turns now. Explain.

▲▲▲▲▲▲▲▲▲▲▲
JUST FOR FUN

▼Watch to see how rollers and wheels are used when a house or other building is moved from one place to another.

Making Rules About Friction

More than 400 years ago, the Italian scientist and artist Leonardo da Vinci (1452–1519) did a number of experiments to try to understand friction. Through the years, many other people have investigated friction, but we still don't understand it thoroughly. However, some sensible patterns have been discovered from the experimental data.

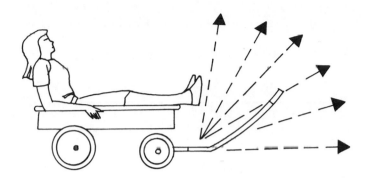

FIGURE 5-7 *Does the angle at which you pull a wagon affect the force you have to apply to make it move?*

The data in Table 5-1 give the results obtained by some experimenters when wooden blocks with different weights were moved across a smooth, wood surface with weights, thread, and a pulley as was shown in Figure 5-1*a*.

TABLE 5-1

Weight of Wooden Block (N)	Approximate Force Needed to Make Block Slide at Constant Speed (N)
1.0	0.3
2.0	0.5
4.0	1.0
5.0	1.3
6.0	1.5
8.0	2.1
10.0	2.6

Can you find a pattern in these data? If you can, use the pattern to predict the force that would be needed to make a 2.5-N block or a 20-N block slide at constant speed.

Sometimes a graph makes it easier to see the pattern. Figure 5-8 is a graph of the data in Table 5-1. Compare the numbers in the table with the points on the graph to see how the graph was made.

Can you predict now the force that would be needed to make a 2.5-N block slide? How about a 20-N block?

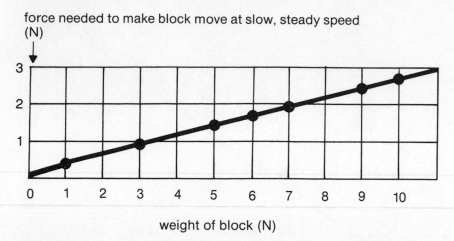

force needed to make block move at slow, steady speed (N)

weight of block (N)

FIGURE 5-8 *A graph of the data in Table 5-1 for wood sliding on wood.*

A similar experiment was done using a block with a rubber surface that was pulled across the same smooth, wood surface. The data from this experiment are shown in Table 5–2.

TABLE 5–2

Weight of Block with a Rubber Surface (N)	Force Needed to Make Block Slide at Constant Speed (N)
1.1	0.7
2.1	1.4
4.1	2.7
6.1	4.2
8.1	5.5
10.1	7.1

Figure 5–9 is a graph of the data in Table 5–2. Compare the pattern in this graph with the one in Figure 5–8. Compare the force needed to slide rubber on wood with the force needed to slide wood on wood, given blocks of the same weight.

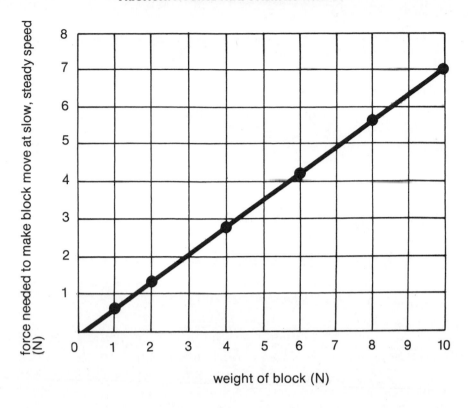

FIGURE 5-9 *A graph of the data in Table 5-2 for rubber sliding on wood.*

If both sets of data were plotted on the same graph, how would the steepness of the two lines compare? What do you think the data for an ice block sliding on wood would look like?

Suppose the force needed to slide the block along at constant speed is divided by the weight of the block. The fraction you would get for wood sliding on wood is about ¼, or 0.25. For rubber sliding on wood, the fraction is about ⅔, or 0.67. We might call these ratios the "friction fractions." Each seems to be reasonably constant. Additional materials give similar results. In fact, physicists and engineers give the friction fraction a special name. They call it the *coefficient of friction*, but we'll continue to call it the friction fraction. The friction fractions for a number of different surfaces are shown in Table 5–3.

TABLE 5–3

Surfaces in Contact	Friction Fraction (Force Needed to Slide Object/Weight of Object)
wood on wood	0.25, or $1/4$
glass on glass	0.90, or $9/10$
steel on steel	0.58, or $58/100$
ice on ice (0° C or 32°F)	0.10, or $1/10$
ice on ice (–12°C or 10°F)	0.30, or $3/10$
ski wax on wet snow (32°F)	0.10, or $1/10$
ski wax on dry snow (32°F)	0.04, or $4/100$
ski wax on dry snow (10°F)	0.20, or $1/5$
brake lining on cast iron	0.40, or $2/5$

In still other experiments, various lubricating liquids were placed between two surfaces to see how they affect friction. Some of the results are shown in Table 5–4.

TABLE 5–4

Surfaces in Contact	Lubricating Liquid	Friction Fraction
steel on steel	none	0.58
steel on steel	castor oil	0.095
steel on steel	olive oil	0.105
steel on steel	light machine oil	0.16
steel on steel	heavy motor oil	0.195
steel on steel	glycerol	0.20
steel on steel	oleic acid	0.08

From the data in the table, can you conclude which of the liquids are good lubricants and which are poor ones? Some of the better lubricants in the table are not used for machines, whereas some of the poorer ones are. Can you explain why?

Other experiments have been done to try to find the effect of surface area on friction. In these experiments, the weight of the block being pulled was kept the same. The kind of material on the surface of the block and the table along which it was moved were kept the same, too. Only the area of the block rubbing on the table was changed. The data for one such experiment are given in Table 5–5.

TABLE 5–5

Surface Area of Wood Block on Smooth, Horizontal Table Top (Square cm)	Force Needed to Move Block at Steady Speed (N)
12.5	1.0
25	1.1
38	1.0
56	1.0
100	1.1

From the data in Table 5–5, what can you conclude about the effect of surface area on friction? By looking back to Table 5–1, see whether you can figure out the weight of the blocks used in collecting the data in Table 5–5. What do you think the data would look like if the block's surface were rubber instead of wood?

▲▲▲▲▲▲▲▲▲▲▲
EXPLORING ON YOUR OWN

▼Find the friction fraction for paper on paper; for paper on wood; for rubber on paper; for other surfaces.

▲▲▲▲▲▲▲▲▲▲▲
JUST FOR FUN

▼Try to imagine what it would be like to live in a frictionless world. In what ways would it be like living in a weightless world? In what ways would it be different?

Friction, Wheels, and Hills

You know from experience that your bike or wagon can roll down a hill despite friction. You've tilted a board and seen the force of gravity overcome the friction between a block and the board. And you know that the more you tilt the board, the greater is the force acting on the block along the surface of the board. Even though the force of gravity pulls you toward the center of the earth, part of that force can pull along an incline such as a hill.

The same sort of thing happens when you pull a wagon at an angle as shown in Figure 5-7. Even though you pull at an angle, the wagon will still move as long as some of the pull is directed forward. Of course, when the pull is straight up, the cart will not move forward because now none of the force is directed forward. In the same way, a wagon will not roll along a level surface even though it is pulled by the earth's gravity. Because gravity acts straight downward, no part of the gravitational force can act in a horizontal direction. However, it can act along inclines, such as hills, roofs, and stairs, because there is a downward component of gravity along such inclines.

In the next investigation, you'll see how inclines affect the forces needed to overcome gravity and friction.

▲▲▲▲▲▲▲▲▲▲▲

INVESTIGATION 5–5: FRICTION, HILLS, AND GRAVITY

Materials needed: smooth blocks (used before) · long, smooth board · one of the first three devices *(a–c)* used to measure friction in Investigation 5–1 · toy truck · books or other, similar objects · large protractor · block with rubber band surface (used before)

Place one of the smooth blocks on the long, smooth, horizontal board and, using one of the first three devices used to measure friction in Investigation 5–1, measure the force needed to make it slide along the board at a steady speed. Now raise one end of the board until the block starts to slide on its own. Lower the board a little so the block no longer slides. Hold the board at that angle as you place some books or other objects under it to support it. Now measure the force needed to move the block *down* the incline. Then measure the force needed to move the block *up* the incline. How does each force compare with the force needed to slide the block along the board when it is level? Can you explain why the forces are all different?

Place the toy truck on the board. Raise the board until the truck starts to move. How steep is the incline when the truck starts to roll? What does this tell you?

Now use the books or other, similar objects to support the board at different angles relative to a level table or floor. You can measure the angles with the protractor. For each angle, measure the force needed to pull the truck up the inclined board at a steady speed. Try measuring the force at angles of 0°, 15°, 30°, 45°, 60°, 75°, and 90° as shown in Figure 5–10. What happens to the force as the angle gets bigger? At what angle is the force needed to move the truck equal to the weight of the truck?

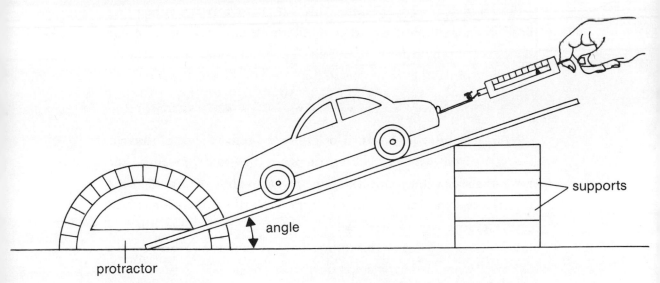

supports

angle

protractor

FIGURE 5-10 *Does the steepness of the hill affect the force you must exert to pull a truck up a "hill"?*

Pull the block with a rubber-band surface up the incline at the same angles you used for the toy truck. Is the force you have to apply to move this block up the hill ever greater than the weight of the block? If it is, how can you explain that fact?

▲▲▲▲▲▲▲▲▲▲▲
EXPLORING ON YOUR OWN

▼From your results in Investigation 5–5, predict the force needed to pull a toy truck dragging a block behind it along a horizontal board. Now place the block on the truck. How much force do you think will be needed to move the truck and block now? Repeat the experiment, using a block that has a rubber-band surface. Can you predict the forces needed now?

▼Suppose you pull a truck and block with a force greater than that needed to overcome friction. What will happen according to the second law of motion? Try it! Does this happen?

▼Some old cars had brakes on only one pair of wheels. After you've tried the following experiments, maybe you'll be able to tell whether the brakes were on the front or rear wheels.

Find a toy car or truck with wheels that turn freely. When you place it on a smooth board and lift the board a little, the car should roll straight down the "hill." Wrap a rubber band around both the front and rear wheels so that none of the wheels can turn. Will the car roll down the hill now? Will it slide down the hill if you make the hill steeper?

Next, use a rubber band to lock only the rear wheels of the car. Leave the front wheels free to turn. Raise the board until the car starts to slide. What happens to the car as it slides down the hill? Repeat the experiment, but this time lock the front wheels and leave the rear wheels free to turn. What happens when the car slides this time? Do you think the front or the rear brakes on a car lock first when a driver steps on the brake pedal? Which set of wheels on old cars should have had brakes?

You've seen that friction is a very important force and that it depends on a number of factors. In the next chapter you will investigate some simple machines. You'll start with a machine called the inclined plane, which is one you have been using in this chapter every time you tilted a board. The inclined plane is one simple machine that humans have used for thousands of years. You'll soon learn the reason for using simple machines.

SIMPLE MACHINES TO MOVE US

One of the reasons we humans have survived as a species is that we have used our brains to devise machines that extend our strength and senses beyond their natural limits. Just as a telescope or microscope can extend our vision, so a machine can increase the strength of the forces we exert.

Most of the machines we use, such as can openers, screw drivers, and pencil sharpeners, are *complex* machines. They are called complex because they are made up of a combination of six *simple* machines. These simple machines are (1) the inclined plane, (2) the wedge, (3) the lever, (4) the pulley, (5) the wheel and axle, and (6) the screw. Two of these, the wedge and the screw, are actually modified forms of the inclined plane. In Figure 6–1, you will find an illustration of each type of simple machine.

You used an inclined plane in Chapter 5 as a way of comparing the friction between different surfaces and as a way of using

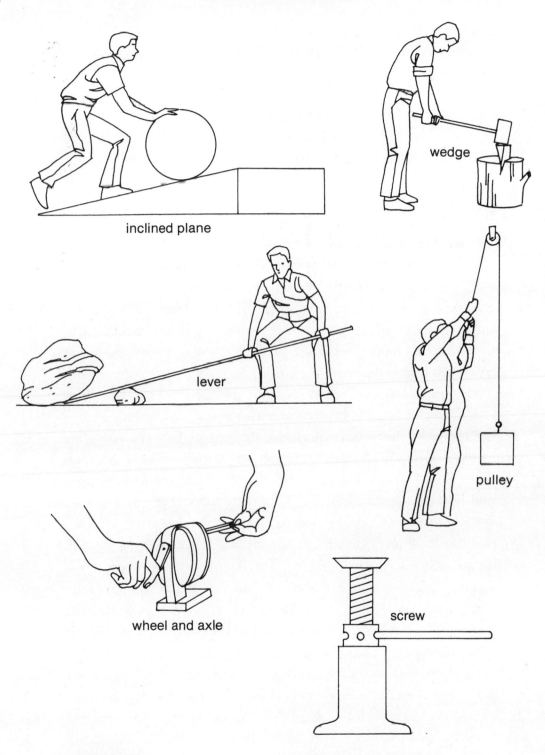

inclined plane

wedge

lever

pulley

wheel and axle

screw

FIGURE 6-1 *Simple machines are useful in a variety of activities.*

gravity to overcome friction. Investigation 6–1 will help you to understand how an inclined plane can change the force needed to do a simple job.

▲▲▲▲▲▲▲▲▲▲▲▲
INVESTIGATION 6–1:
THE INCLINED PLANE—A SIMPLE MACHINE

Materials needed: spring scale · toy truck · long, smooth board · wagon · tie bands (twist ties)

Use the spring scale to measure the weight of the toy truck. Then place the truck on the long, smooth board raised at one end to make an angle of about 30° with the floor or table. You can use one of the tie bands to attach the spring scale to the truck. Use the spring scale to measure the force needed to pull the truck slowly up the incline. How does this force compare with the weight of the truck? How does an inclined plane make it easier to lift an object?

Do you do less work when you roll an object up an incline than you do when you lift it? In order to answer this question, you need to know that in science *work* is defined as the force acting on an object times the distance through which the force acts. You can easily find the work done in lifting the toy truck you used. Simply multiply the weight of the truck by the height of the incline (the vertical distance from the floor or table to the top of the incline) (see Figure 6–2). For example, if the truck weighs 5 N and the height is 30 cm, the work done is 150 N-cm.

The work done in rolling the truck up the incline is equal to the force needed to pull it along the incline times the length of the incline. The force is less in this case but the distance is greater. If the force to pull the truck along the incline is 3 N and the length of the incline is 60 cm, the work done is 180 N-cm. From your own data, how does the work done in lifting the truck to the top of the incline compare with the work done in rolling it up the incline? Were the two values for work about the same?

If the work done to move a heavy weight along an incline is

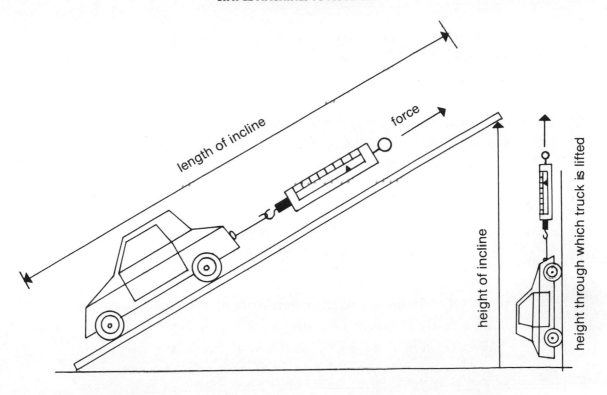

FIGURE 6-2 *Here are two ways to do the same job. Is the work done the same?*

greater than the work to lift it straight up to the top of the incline, what is the point of using the incline? (Hint: Think in terms of the force needed.)

Now turn the truck over (upside down) and pull it up the incline. What force is required to drag the truck up the incline? How does the work done in dragging the truck along the incline compare with the work done in rolling the truck up the incline? How do you account for the difference?

▲▲▲▲▲▲▲▲▲▲▲▲
EXPLORING ON YOUR OWN

▼How much work do you have to do to climb to the top of a playground slide? How much work is required to pull you up along the slide itself? With a strong spring balance or a bathroom scale, **an adult can measure the force needed to pull you along the slide.**

▼The thread of a screw is like an inclined plane wrapped around a rod. The slope of the incline in a screw can be determined from the number of threads per centimeter or inch. Find two screws that have the same diameter but a different number of threads per centimeter. Which screw do you think will be easier to turn with a screwdriver? What can you do to test your prediction?

▲▲▲▲▲▲▲▲▲▲▲
JUST FOR FUN

▼Show that the wedge and the screw are both types of inclined planes. For example, wind a long triangle of paper in spiral fashion around a wooden cylinder, as shown in Figure 6–3.

▼You use an inclined plane to make work easier every time you walk up a flight of stairs. Make a list of other places where you see inclined planes being used to make work easier.

Work and Power

Work is the product of force and the distance an object moves while acted upon by the force. The rate at which work is done is called *power*. If you do a great deal of work in a short time, the power you develop is great. If you do the same work more slowly, you develop less power.

The Scottish inventor James Watt (1736–1819) measured power in terms of the work an average horse could do at a steady rate. He found that such a horse could do 550 foot-pounds (ft lb) of work in one second. That is, it could lift a 100 lb. weight, by means of a rope and pulley, through a height of 5.5 ft. in 1 s, or a 550 lb. weight through a height of 1 ft. in 1 s. (In each case, the product of *feet* and *pounds* is equal to 550.) This unit of power became known as the *horsepower* (abbreviation: *HP*). One horsepower equals 550 ft lb/s. Later, a unit of power was named in

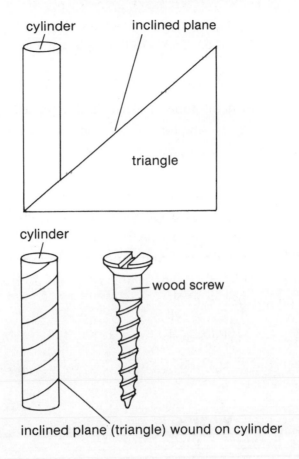

cylinder

inclined plane

triangle

cylinder

wood screw

inclined plane (triangle) wound on cylinder

FIGURE 6-3 *When you wrap an inclined plane (a triangle) around a cylinder (a) you get a spiraled inclined plane (b) that resembles a wood screw (c).*

honor of Watt. A *watt* is smaller than a horsepower. In fact, it takes 746 watts to equal one horsepower.

In the next investigation, you'll measure the power that you can develop over a short period of time.

▲▲▲▲▲▲▲▲▲▲▲

INVESTIGATION 6–2: HOW POWERFUL ARE YOU?

Materials needed: yardstick or measuring tape · bathroom scale · stopwatch (or wristwatch with a stopwatch mode)

To find out how much power you can develop, you can measure how long it takes you to lift your own weight up a flight of stairs of known height. The force you exert is the force needed to lift your own weight from the floor to the ceiling. To begin, use the yardstick, or measuring tape to measure the vertical height from the base of the stairs to the top. If you don't know how much you weigh, use the bathroom scale to find out. Finally, you'll need someone to use the stopwatch to measure how long it takes you to (1) walk up the stairs; and (2) run up the stairs.

To find your power, you need to know how much work you did and how long it took you to do it. For example, suppose you weigh 100 lbs., and the vertical height from the bottom to the top of the stairs is 10 ft. If it takes you 4.0 s to go up the stairs, the work you do is 1,000 ft lb:

$$100 \text{ lb.} \times 10 \text{ ft.} = 1,000 \text{ ft lb}$$

Since you did that work in 4.0 s, the power you developed is 250 ft lb/s, or 0.45 hp:

$$\frac{1,000 \text{ ft lb}}{4.0 \text{ s}} = 250 \text{ ft lb/s}$$

$$\frac{250 \text{ ft lb}}{550 \text{ ft lb/hp}} = 0.45 \text{ hp}$$

From your own data, how much power, in foot-pounds and in horsepower, did you develop when you walked up the stairs? When you ran up the stairs? If possible, compare your results with those of friends who did the same experiment. You might also ask a number of adults or high-school-age students to try this experiment. Compare their weight and the power they can develop. Does a person's weight seem to affect the power he or she can develop?

The Lever: Another Simple Machine

One of the oldest machines is the lever. The ancient Greek

scientist Archimedes (287–212 B.C.) was the first person to work out a mathematical explanation of how the lever works. In describing the lever, he is reported to have said: "Give me a place to stand and I can move the world." Archimedes knew that by applying a small force at a great enough distance from the *fulcrum*, or point about which the lever turns, he could move a heavy object that was close to the fulcrum. Figure 6-4 shows the basic form of the lever and the names for the forces and distances that are used in describing levers. The *effort arm* is the distance from the fulcrum to the point where a force (*the effort force*) is applied to do some work. The *resistance arm* is the distance from the fulcrum to the *resistance force*, or load that opposes the effort force.

Color Plate IX shows some examples of levers. Can you diagram these levers the way the lever is diagrammed in Figure 6-4? Levers are very commonly used machines; you'll see them in many places. During Investigation 6–3, you'll have a chance to experiment with levers and build a balance that is really a lever that has been modified to weigh things.

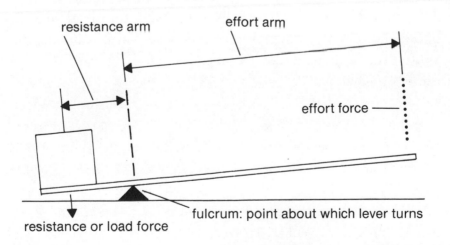

FIGURE 6-4 *The lever is among the oldest of machines. This diagram shows the basic form of the lever and illustrates the distribution of forces along the lever.*

▲▲▲▲▲▲▲▲▲▲▲

INVESTIGATION 6–3: LEVERS AND BALANCES

Materials needed: wooden ruler · pencil · book · pin · two drinking glasses or cans · plastic soda straws · paper clips

Use the wooden ruler and the pencil as a lever and fulcrum as shown in Figure 6–5a. Support the book at one end of the ruler. Let the book's weight push on the end of the ruler. Use your hand only to prevent the book from falling over. Press on the other end of the ruler with your finger to lift the book. Move the pencil (fulcrum) to a point near the end of the ruler where the book is located. Lift the book again by pressing down on the opposite end of the ruler, as shown in Figure 6–5b. Finally, place the fulcrum near the end where you push down (Figure 6–5c), and again lift the book by pushing down with your finger.

In which case was it easiest to lift the book? In which case was it hardest? How does the ratio of the effort arm to the resistance arm affect the size of the effort force needed to lift the same object?

To build another simple lever, place the ends of the pin on the edges of the two drinking glasses or cans as shown in Figure 6–6a. The pin will serve as a fulcrum for your lever. Try to balance one of the plastic soda straws on the fulcrum so that it is horizontal. Why is this so hard to do? (Remember what you learned about center of mass!)

Next, try to balance the soda straw after pushing the pin through the center of mass of the straw. (You might want to try balancing the straw on your finger first to find the right place.) Should you put the pin near the middle or near one end of the straw? Should you put it through the middle, bottom, or top of the straw (see Figure 6–6b)? Which pin position makes the straw easiest to balance? Will the straw stay balanced if you turn it over (upside down)? If you turn it around (end for end)?

Hang one of the paper clips near one end of the balanced straw. (If the clip slides along the straw, you may have to bend it together

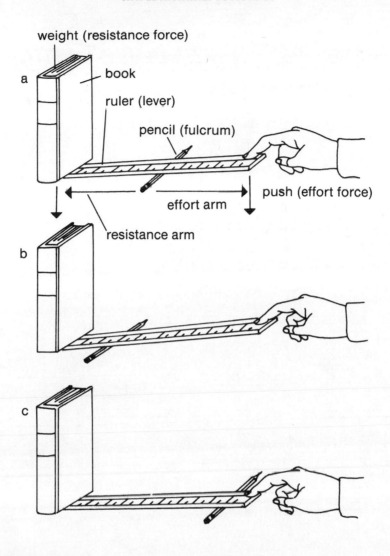

FIGURE 6-5 *Experimenting with a simple lever.*

a little so it will stay in place.) Where should you place a paper clip on the other end of the straw to make it balance (stay horizontal)? The drawings in Figure 6-6c show some paper clips on the left side of the straw balance. For each case shown, what do you have to do to the right side of the straw to make the straw balance? Is there more than one way to make it balance? For example, in how many of the cases shown can you balance the straw by using just one paper clip on the right side? For how

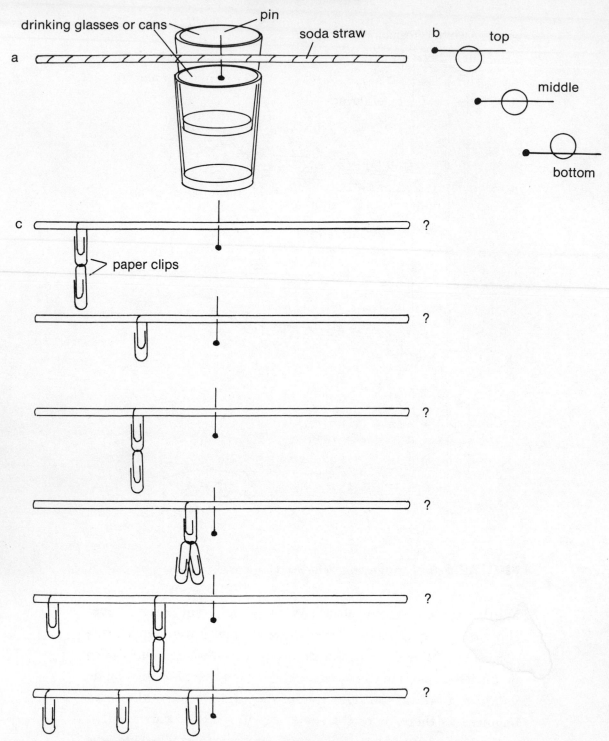

FIGURE 6-6 *You can build and experiment with a soda-straw lever that is actually a balance. See the text for details.*

many cases can you make it balance using two paper clips on the right side? Three paper clips on the right? Four? More than four?

Continue to experiment with your soda-straw balance, using paper clips on each side. Can you discover a rule that allows you to predict how to balance the straw, given a certain maximum number of paper clips that you may add to the right side? Are there some cases in which you can predict that the straw will not balance unless you can use more paper clips than the maximum number allotted?

Once you think you have discovered a rule, ask a partner to set up the left side of the balance with paper clips. Then predict where you can place a fixed number of paper clips to make the beam balance. Test your prediction. Does your rule work?

▲▲▲▲▲▲▲▲▲▲▲
EXPLORING ON YOUR OWN

▼You can build a very good balance with a plastic soda straw, common pins, scissors, thread, small or cut-off paper cups or soufflé cups, tape, paper clips, tongue depressors, books, rubber bands, and a small piece of clay. Begin by cutting a narrow slit about 1 cm long at each end of the straw (Figure 6–7a). Turn the straw so that the slits face downward (Figure 6–7b). Stick one pin through the straw at a point just above the straw's center of gravity. This pin will serve as the fulcrum (Figure 6–7c). Now stick pins through the straw exactly 0.5 cm in from each end. The pins should be directly above the center of the narrow slits and no higher than the midpoint of the straw. Put a tiny piece of tape over each point so you won't get cut. Small paper clips can be slipped into the slits and over the pins. Set up the straw as shown in Figure 6–7d. The paper clips can be used to suspend paper balance pans from the pins. If the beam is not level, add a small piece of clay to the lighter side.

You can now use the balance to weigh a variety of small objects by seeing how many gram masses you must place in the right-

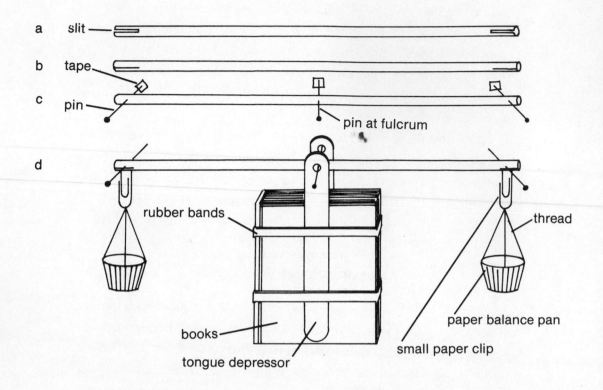

a   slit

b   tape

c   pin

pin at fulcrum

d

rubber bands

thread

books

paper balance pan

tongue depressor

small paper clip

FIGURE 6-7 *Building and using a soda-straw balance.*

hand pan to balance the object in the left-hand pan. If you don't
have a set of gram masses, you can use identical paper clips or
small washers as your unit of mass. First find the number of
paper clips or washers in a gram. To do this, use the balance to
determine the number of paper clips or washers whose mass is
equal to that of a nickel. A nickel weighs just about 5 g. Then
divide the number of washers or paper clips by 5 to find the
number in one gram.

Can you figure out a way to measure fractions of a gram on
your balance? How accurate can you make the balance?

▼Figure 6–8 shows a balance made from two simple machines. This balance can weigh very small masses. First, push a small machine screw about halfway into one end of a plastic soda straw. Then balance the straw and screw on your finger. Put a pin through the straw at the balance point. The pin will serve as the fulcrum. Be sure the pin is just above the vertical midpoint of the straw. Cut out a small piece from the top of the end of the straw opposite the machine screw. The resulting space will serve as a small pan for your balance.

To calibrate your balance, place the fulcrum on a pair of glass microscope slides as shown in Figure 6–8. Turn the machine screw, moving it deeper into the straw, until the opposite end of the beam tilts up at an angle of about 30° with the horizontal. Weigh a sheet of graph paper on a balance calibrated in grams. Then calculate the mass of one small square of the paper. For example, if the sheet weighs 1 g and contains 100 squares, each square must weigh 1/100, or 0.01 g.

Use a clothespin to support a file card or a sheet of cardboard on the table, next to the pan of your balance. Mark the position of the pan on the card. Then put a known mass of paper squares on the pan. Mark the new level of the pan on the card. Next to the mark write the mass that corresponds to this position. Repeat this for a number of small masses.

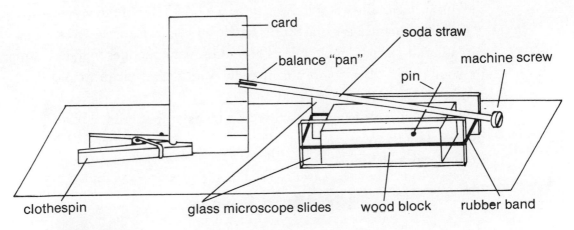

FIGURE 6-8 *A small but sensitive balance can be built from a soda straw.*

What range of masses can you read with this balance? What is useful about the balance? What are its weaknesses? See whether you can build a balance that is as accurate as this one but does not have its weaknesses.

▼Do you think you weigh more standing up or lying down? Or do you think you weigh the same either way? To find out, place on a bathroom scale a board about as long as you are tall. Have someone record the weight of you and the board when you lie on the board. Then find your weight when you stand on the board. What do you conclude?

▼You might like to investigate what your weight is when it is spread out over two bathroom scales. Use the same board you just did, but have one end of the board rest on one scale and the other end on a second scale. Have a partner record the readings on both scales when you stand at different places on the board. What do you find? What do you find if you move the scales to different positions under the board?

▲▲▲▲▲▲▲▲▲▲▲
JUST FOR FUN

▼Look at the huge lever shown in Color Plate X. This lever can be found at the Franklin Institute Science Museum in Philadelphia. Notice that the person pulling on the rope farthest out from the fulcrum can lift a 500-lb. weight at the other end of the lever.

▼Building mobiles is an art form based on the lever. Use wires, thread, and various small objects to build several mobiles to hang in your room. Let your imagination and the lever principle you've discovered serve as guides.

▼You use a simple lever every time you transfer food from a plate to your mouth. Make a list of the levers you see elsewhere—for example, in machines.

Modified Levers

The principle of the inclined plane can be modified to make

screws and wedges. Similarly, the principle of the lever is used in pulleys and in wheels and axles. In the next two investigations, you'll see how your knowledge of levers can be used to understand these two other simple machines.

▲▲▲▲▲▲▲▲▲▲▲
INVESTIGATION 6–3: PULLEYS

Materials needed: spring scale · one or more pulleys (or spools and wire) · weight · string · double pulleys (if possible)

Use the spring scale to weigh the weight. Then attach a pulley to the hook or secure it in some way, as shown in the Figure 6–9*a* setup, so that you can use a pulley to lift the weight. Connect the weight to the spring scale by running a string over the pulley, as shown in the same drawing. (If you don't have a pulley, you can use a spool suspended from a wire that runs through the hole in the center of the spool.) Notice the similarity between the pulley and a lever. Why is this pulley like an equal-arm balance? How does the effort force that you exert downward compare with the weight of the object that is pulled upward? Does this pulley change the strength of the force, the direction of the force, or both?

Now connect the pulley to the weight, as shown in the Figure 6–9*b* setup. Again, note the similarity between this pulley system and a lever. Then see whether you can predict how the effort force you apply with the spring scale will compare with the weight of the object lifted. Try it! Was your prediction correct?

If you have two pulleys, try a setup like the one in Figure 6–9*c*. Notice that three strings are now pulling upward on the weight. See whether you can predict the approximate force that will be recorded on the spring scale. Why is the pulley setup shown in Figure 6–9*d* called a "fool's pulley"? (Hint: What will happen when the effort force is applied?)

If you have double pulleys (two wheels side by side in a pulley frame), see how the effort force changes as you use more and

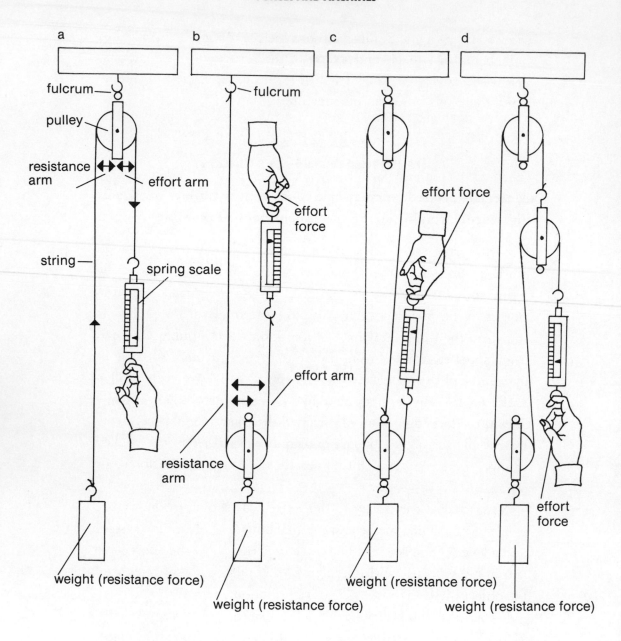

FIGURE 6-9 *You can build several different pulley setups to investigate how a pulley works.*

more strings to lift the weight. Can such pulleys change both the direction of the force and the strength of the force needed to lift something?

▲▲▲▲▲▲▲▲▲▲▲
EXPLORING ON YOUR OWN

▼The gears, pedals, and chain on your bike make up a machine that is a combination of simple and modified simple machines. What are these simple and modified simple machines? How do they work? What happens when you shift gears on your bike? Which combination magnifies your force the most? The least?

▼You can make the simple multiple-pulley system shown in Figure 6–10, using two strong wooden dowels and a length of rope. If two friends pull hard outward on the dowels, you'll still be able to pull the sticks together simply by pulling rather gently on the free end of the rope. How is the strength of your pull related to the number of loops around the dowels?

▲▲▲▲▲▲▲▲▲▲▲
JUST FOR FUN

▼Make a list of all the places where you see pulleys being used to change the direction or strength of a force. You'll find lots of them around construction sites and car-repair shops.

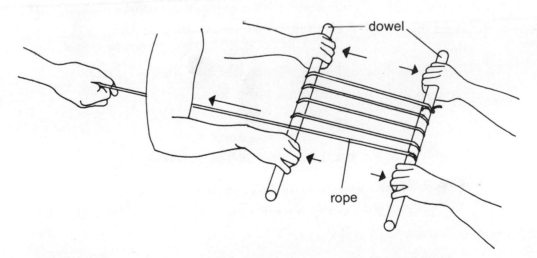

FIGURE 6-10 *How is the strength of the pull on the dowels related to the number of loops around the dowels in this multiple-pulley system?*

▲▲▲▲▲▲▲▲▲▲▲
INVESTIGATION 6–4: WHEEL AND AXLE

Materials needed: tape · heavy wire (coat hanger) · dowel · weight, such as a book or fishing sinker · spring scale · tacks · pliers

Assemble the simple wheel and axle shown in Figure 6–11, using the dowel, heavy wire (coat hanger), pieces of wood, string, tape, tacks, and pliers. Make the wheel by taping the bent wire to the dowel. The handle, since it goes around can be considered as a wheel with only one spoke. **Be sure to tape the end of the wire handle to avoid cuts.** (If you don't have these materials, you can take a rotary pencil sharpener apart and use it. Alternatively, you might consider using Tinker Toy parts or the wheel and axle on a toy car or truck.)

Notice the similarity between the wheel and a lever (see the end view in Figure 6–11). Attach the weight to the axle. The weight is the resistance force. Turn the handle (wheel) by pulling gently with the spring scale to measure the effort force. How does the effort force compare with the resistance force?

If possible, use a "wheel" with a larger diameter—that is, a longer handle. If you're using the heavy wire handle as a wheel, bend the wire so the handle is farther out from the axle. How does the increase in diameter affect the effort force? When you use a larger wheel, what happens to the distance you have to move your hand to make the axle turn around once?

▲▲▲▲▲▲▲▲▲▲▲
EXPLORING ON YOUR OWN

▼Draw some gears on cardboard. Use scissors to cut the gears out. Pins can be used to mount the gears on a large sheet of wood or cardboard. Make a set of two gears in such a way that the second gear will turn twice as fast as the first one. Then make a set of three gears in which the third gear is to turn in the same

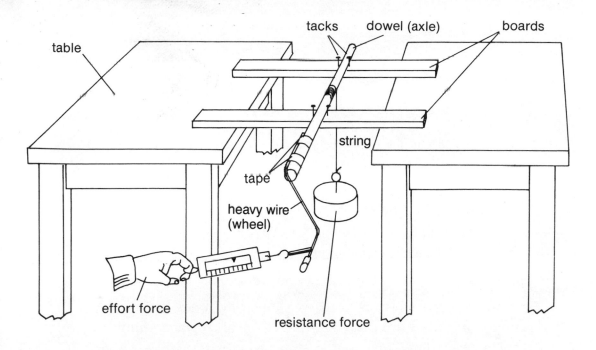

tacks   dowel (axle)   boards

table

string

tape

heavy wire
(wheel)

effort force

resistance force

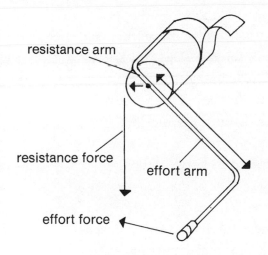

resistance arm

resistance force   effort arm

effort force

enlarged end view of wheel and axle

FIGURE 6-11 *This setup can be used to investigate the properties of the wheel and axle.*

direction as the first gear but only half as fast. Experiment with a variety of gear sets of your own design.

▲▲▲▲▲▲▲▲▲▲▲
JUST FOR FUN

▼Make a list of places where you find wheels and axles that are used to change the strength of a force.

▼Use a variety of simple machines to build your own toy car. The simplest way to "power" your car is to use an inclined plane. However, it might be more fun to use twisted rubber bands and a weight or a small electric motor.

You've seen that there are six simple machines but that the wedge and screw are really forms of the inclined plane. Similarly, the pulley and the wheel and axle may be seen as modified levers.

If you visit the Franklin Institute Science Museum or a similar hands-on museum in your area, you'll be able to see and operate some of these simple machines. In addition, these museums will keep you abreast of new developments in science. Did you know, for example, that researchers at the University of California at Berkeley are developing devices called *microbots*? These are tiny robots with gears no wider than a hair. Eventually they may be used to "bulldoze" away the fatty deposits in arteries or carry medicine to a precise position inside a person's body.

Developing machines the size of body cells or of giant molecules may one day be possible. Such tiny machines may prove as valuable as the giant machines that have carried us into space. Just as giant rockets have enabled us to move outward and explore the vast expanse of space, so these tiny machines may enable us to move inward and explore the cells that make up living organisms and the atoms that constitute matter. This will become possible through applying a knowledge of forces and machines—a knowledge you've now come a long way toward acquiring.

▲▲▲▲▲▲▲▲▲▲▲

BIBLIOGRAPHY

Beiser, Germaine. *The Story of Gravity.* New York: Dutton, 1968.

Brown, Bob. *Science for You: 112 Illustrated Experiments.* Blue Ridge Summit, Pa.: Tab Books, 1988.

Carrying Energy. Englewood Cliffs, N.J.: Silver Burdett Press, 1989.

Cohen, Lynn. *Energy & Machines.* Palo Alto, Calif.: Monday Morning Books, 1988.

Conway, Lorraine. *Energy.* Carthage, Ill.: Good Apple, 1985.

Gardner, Robert. *Science and Sports.* New York: Watts, 1988.

Gardner, Robert. *Science Around the House.* New York: Messner, 1985.

Gardner, Robert, and David Webster. *Science in Your Backyard.* New York: Messner, 1986.

Herbert, Don. *Mr. Wizard's Supermarket Science.* New York: Random House, 1980.

Laithwarte, Eric. *Force: The Power Behind Movement.* New York: Watts, 1986.

Neal, Philip. *Energy Power Source and Electricity*. Pomfret, Vt: David and Charles, 1989.

Ward, Alan. *Experimenting with Energy*. Pomfret, Vt.: David and Charles, 1988.

Webster, David. *Brain-Boosters*. New York: Natural History Press, 1966.

———. *More Brain-Boosters*. New York: Doubleday, 1975.

———. *Towers*. New York: Natural History Press, 1971.

Wood, Robert W. *Physics for Kids: 49 Easy Experiments with Mechanics*. Blue Ridge Summit, Pa.: Tab Books, 1989.

▲▲▲▲▲▲▲▲▲▲▲

PHOTO ACKNOWLEDGMENTS

Jim Abbott: Plate II (top and bottom), Plate X. Don Carroll/The Image Bank: Plate III. A Chopra/PRJ: Plate VIII. Great Adventure: Plate I. Paul Metzger/Photo Researchers: Plate V. Stephen Mullen: Plate IX (all). NASA: Plate VI. Mike Shaw: Plate IV. Jerry Wachter/Photo Researchers: Plate VII.

▲▲▲▲▲▲▲▲▲▲▲

INDEX

▲▲▲▲▲▲▲▲▲▲

ABOUT THE AUTHOR

Robert Gardner has written more than thirty books for children of all ages, including *Kitchen Chemistry, Science Around the House, Science in Your Backyard* (with David Webster), *Projects in Space Science, The Whale Watchers' Guide, The Young Athlete's Manual,* and *The Future and the Past* (with Dennis Shortelle), all of which were published by Julian Messner. For many years he was chairman of the science department at the Salisbury School in Salisbury, Connecticut, where he taught chemistry, biology, and physical science. For three years during the 1960s he was a staff member of both the Elementary Science Study and the Physical Science Group at the Education Development Center in Newton, Massachusetts, where he worked on several National Science Foundation-funded projects involving the development of science materials. He now lives on Cape Cod, where he spends most of his time writing.